1.65

HALLUCINOGENIC PLANTS

by

RICHARD EVANS SCHULTES

Illustrated by
ELMER W. SMITH

 GOLDEN PRESS · NEW YORK
Western Publishing Company, Inc.
Racine, Wisconsin

FOREWORD

Hallucinogenic plants have been used by man for thousands of years, probably since he began gathering plants for food. The hallucinogens have continued to receive the attention of civilized man through the ages. Recently, we have gone through a period during which sophisticated Western society has "discovered" hallucinogens, and some sectors of that society have taken up, for one reason or another, the use of such plants. This trend may be destined to continue.

It is, therefore, important for us to learn as much as we can about hallucinogenic plants. A great body of scientific literature has been published about their uses and their effects, but the information is often locked away in technical journals. The interested layman has a right to sound information on which to base his opinions. This book has been written partly to provide that kind of information.

No matter whether we believe that man's intake of hallucinogens in primitive or sophisticated societies constitutes use, misuse, or abuse, hallucinogenic plants have undeniably played an extensive role in human culture and probably shall continue to do so. It follows that a clear understanding of these physically and socially potent agents should be a part of man's general education.

R. E. S.

CONTENTS

Hallucinogenic plants have been featured on many postage stamps:
(1, 6) *Amanita muscaria*, (2) fruit of *Peganum harmala*, (3) *Atropa belladonna*, (4) *Pancratium trianthum*, (5) *Rivea corymbosa*, (7) *Datura stramonium*, (8) *Datura candida*, (9) *Hyoscyamus niger*.

WHAT ARE
HALLUCINOGENIC PLANTS?

In his search for food, early man tried all kinds of plants. Some nourished him, some, he found, cured his ills, and some killed him. A few, to his surprise, had strange effects on his mind and body, seeming to carry him into other worlds. We call these plants hallucinogens, because they distort the senses and usually produce hallucinations —experiences that depart from reality. Although most hallucinations are visual, they may also involve the senses of hearing, touch, smell, or taste—and occasionally several senses simultaneously are involved.

The actual causes of such hallucinations are chemical substances in the plants. These substances are true narcotics. Contrary to popular opinion, not all narcotics are dangerous and addictive. Strictly and etymologically speaking, a narcotic is any substance that has a depressive effect, whether slight or great, on the central nervous system.

Narcotics that induce hallucinations are variously called hallucinogens (hallucination generators), psychotomimetics (psychosis mimickers), psychotaraxics (mind disturbers), and psychedelics (mind manifesters). No one term fully satisfies scientists, but hallucinogens comes closest. Psychedelic is most widely used in the United States, but it combines two Greek roots incorrectly, is biologically unsound, and has acquired popular meanings beyond the drugs or their effects.

In the history of mankind, hallucinogens have probably been the most important of all the narcotics. Their fantastic effects made them sacred to primitive man and may even have been responsible for suggesting to him the idea of deity.

Paramount among the hallucinogens of religious significance is the peyote cactus. This illustration, called "Morning Prayer in a Peyote Ceremony," is adapted from a painting by Tsa Toke, a Kiowa Indian. These Indians are ritual users of peyote. Central fire and crescent-shaped altar are flanked by ceremonial eagle-feather fans; feathers symbolize morning, and the birds, rising prayers.

HALLUCINOGENS IN PRIMITIVE SOCIETIES

Hallucinogens permeate nearly every aspect of life in primitive societies. They play roles in health and sickness, peace and war, home life and travel, hunting and agriculture; they affect relations among individuals, villages, and tribes. They are believed to influence life before birth and after death.

MEDICAL AND RELIGIOUS USES of hallucinogenic plants are particularly important in primitive societies. Aboriginal people attribute sickness and health to the working of spirit forces. Consequently, any "medicine" that can transport man to the spirit world is considered by many aborigines to be better than one with purely physical effects.

Psychic powers have also been attributed to hallucinogens and have become an integral part of primitive religions. All over the world hallucinogenic plants are used as holy mediators between man and his gods. The prophecies of the oracle of Delphi, for example, are thought to have been induced through hallucinogens.

Makuna Indian medicine man under influence of caapi (aya-huasca or yajé) prepared from bark of *Banisteriopsis caapi.*

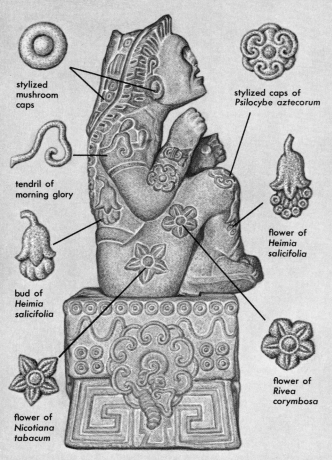

stylized
mushroom
caps

stylized caps of
Psilocybe aztecorum

tendril of
morning glory

flower of
*Heimia
salicifolia*

bud of
*Heimia
salicifolia*

flower of
*Nicotiana
tabacum*

flower of
*Rivea
corymbosa*

Statue of Xochipilli, the Aztec "Prince of Flowers," unearthed in
Tlalmanalco on the slopes of the volcano Popocatepetl and now on
display in the Museo Nacional in Mexico City. Labels indicate
probable botanical interpretation of stylized glyphs.

OTHER ABORIGINAL USES of hallucinogens vary from one primitive culture to another. Many hallucinogenic plants are basic to the initiation rituals of adolescents. The Algonquin Indians gave an intoxicating medicine, wysoccan, to their young men, who then became violently deranged for 20 days. During this period, they lost all memory, starting manhood by forgetting they had been boys. The iboga root in Gabon and caapi in the Amazon are also used in such rituals.

In South America, many tribes take ayahuasca to foresee the future, settle disputes, decipher enemy plans, cast or remove spells, or insure the fidelity of their women. Sensations of death and separation of body and soul are sometimes experienced during a dreamlike trance.

The hallucinogenic properties of *Datura* have been thoroughly exploited, particularly in the New World. In Mexico and in the Southwest, *Datura* is used in divination, prophecy, and ritualistic curing.

Modern Mexican Indians value certain mushrooms as sacraments and use morning glories and the peyote cactus to predict the future, diagnose and cure disease, and placate good and evil spirits.

The Mixtecs of Mexico eat puffballs to hear voices from heaven that answer their questions. The Waikás of Brazil and Venezuela snuff the powdered resin of a jungle tree to ritualize death, induce a trance for diagnosing disease, and thank the spirits for victory in war. The Witotos of Colombia eat the same powerful resin to "talk with the little people." Peruvian medicine men drink cimora to make themselves owners of another's identity. Indians of eastern Brazil drink jurema to have glorious visions of the spirit world before going into battle with their enemies.

USE IN MODERN WESTERN WORLD

Our modern society has recently taken up the use, sometimes illegally, of hallucinogens on a grand scale. Many people believe they can achieve "mystic" or "religious" experience by altering the chemistry of the body with hallucinogens, seldom realizing that they are merely reverting to the age-old practices of primitive societies. Whether drug-induced adventures can be

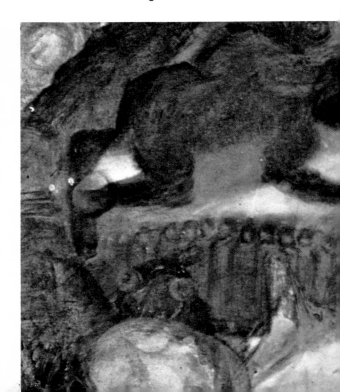

identical with the metaphysical insight claimed by some mystics, or are merely a counterfeit of it, is still controversial. The widespread and expanding use of hallucinogens in our society may have little or no value and may sometimes even be harmful or dangerous. In any event, it is a newly imported and superimposed cultural trait without natural roots in modern Western tradition.

Detail of a painting of a primitive ayahuasca vision by Yando del Rios, contemporary Peruvian artist.

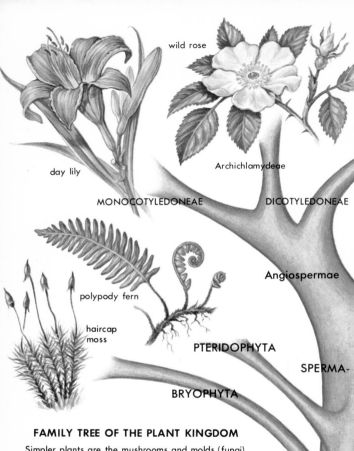

wild rose

day lily

Archichlamydeae

MONOCOTYLEDONEAE

DICOTYLEDONEAE

Angiospermae

polypody fern

haircap
moss

PTERIDOPHYTA

SPERMA-

BRYOPHYTA

FAMILY TREE OF THE PLANT KINGDOM

Simpler plants are the mushrooms and molds (fungi),
seaweeds (algae), mosses and liverworts (bryo-
phytes), and ferns (pteridophytes). More complex
are the seed plants (spermatophytes), subdivided
into cone-bearers (gymnosperms) and flower-bearers
(angiosperms), with one seed leaf (monocots) or two
(dicots), with petals absent or separate (archichlamydeae) or petals joined (metachlamydeae).

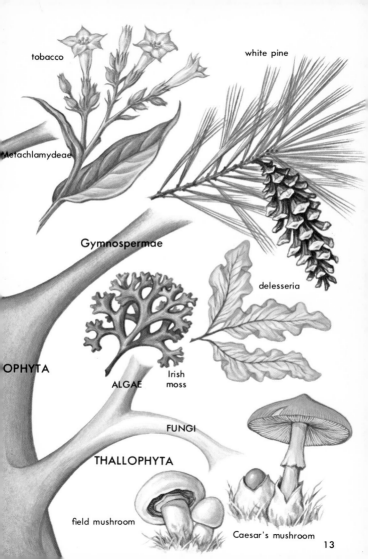

tobacco

white pine

Metachlamydeae

Gymnospermae

delesseria

OPHYTA

ALGAE

Irish
moss

FUNGI

THALLOPHYTA

field mushroom

Caesar's mushroom

13

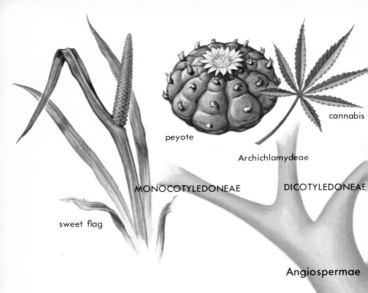

cannabis

peyote

Archichlamydeae

MONOCOTYLEDONEAE

DICOTYLEDONEAE

sweet flag

Angiospermae

PTERIDOPHYTA

SPERMA

BRYOPHYTA

DISTRIBUTION OF HALLUCINOGENS

The majority of hallucinogenic species occur among the highly evolved flowering plants and in one division (fungi) of the simpler, spore-bearing plants. No hallucinogenic species are yet known from the other "branches" of the plant kingdom (see pp. 12–13). Plants illustrated are representative psycho-active species.

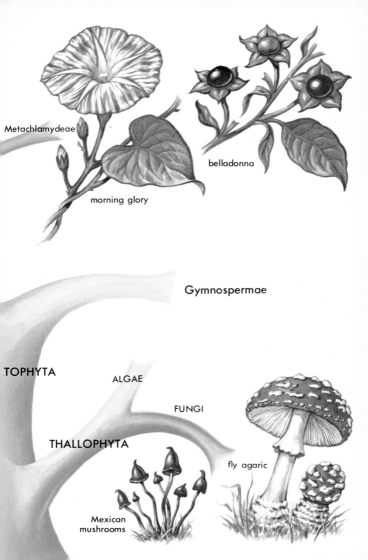

Metachlamydeae

belladonna

morning glory

Gymnospermae

TOPHYTA

ALGAE

FUNGI

THALLOPHYTA

fly agaric

Mexican mushrooms

CHEMICAL COMPOSITION

Hallucinogens are limited to a small number of types of chemical compounds. All hallucinogens found in plants are organic compounds—that is, they contain carbon as an essential part of their structure and were formed in the life processes of vegetable organisms. No inorganic plant constituents, such as minerals, are known to have hallucinogenic effects.

Hallucinogenic compounds may be divided conveniently into two broad groups: those that contain nitrogen in their structure and those that do not. Those with nitrogen are far more common. The most important of those lacking nitrogen are the active principles of marihuana, terpenophenolic compounds classed as dibenzopyrans and called cannabinols—in particular, tetrahydrocannabinols. The hallucinogenic compounds with nitrogen in their structure are alkaloids or related bases.

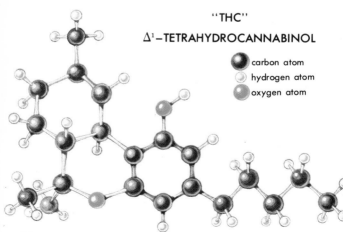

"THC"

Δ^1–TETRAHYDROCANNABINOL

- carbon atom
- hydrogen atom
- oxygen atom

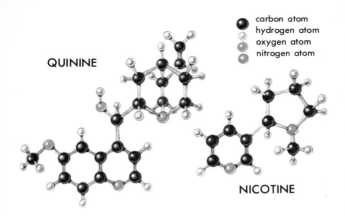

QUININE

carbon atom
hydrogen atom
oxygen atom
nitrogen atom

NICOTINE

ALKALOIDS are a diverse group of some 5,000 compounds with complex molecular structures. They contain nitrogen as well as carbon, oxygen, and hydrogen. All alkaloids are of plant origin, though some proto-alkaloids occur in animals. All are slightly alkaline, hence their name. They are classified into series based on their structures. Many hallucinogenic alkaloids are indoles (see below) or are related to indoles, and the majority have or may have originated in the plant from the amino acid known as tryptophan.

Most medicinal and toxic plants, as well as hallucinogenic plants, owe their biological activity to alkaloids. Examples of widely valued alkaloids are morphine, quinine, nicotine, strychnine, and caffeine.

INDOLES are hallucinogenic alkaloids or related bases, all of them nitrogen-containing compounds. It is most surprising that of the many thousands of organic compounds that act on various parts of the body so few are hallucinogenic. The indole nucleus of the hallucinogens frequently appears in the form of tryptamine derivatives. It is composed of phenyl and pyrrol segments (see diagram on opposite page).

Tryptamines may be "simple"—that is, without substitutions—or they may have various "side chains" known as hydroxy (OH), methoxy (CH_3), or phosphogloxy (OPO_3H) groups in the phenyl ring.

The indole ring (shown in red in the diagram) is evident not only in the numerous tryptamines (dimethyltryptamine, etc.) but also in the various ergoline alkaloids (ergine and others), in the ibogaine alkaloids, and in the β-carboline alkaloids (harmine, harmaline, etc.). Lysergic acid diethylamide (LSD) has an indole nucleus. One reason for the significance of the indolic hallucinogens may be their structural similarity to the neurohumoral tryptamine serotonin (5-hydroxydimethyltryptamine), present in the nervous tissue of warm-blooded animals. Serotonin plays a major role in the biochemistry of the central nervous system. A study of the functioning of hallucinogenic tryptamine may experimentally help to explain the function of serotonin in the body.

A chemical relationship similar to that between indolic hallucinogens and serotonin exists between mescaline, an hallucinogenic phenylethylamine base in peyote, and the neurohormone norepinephrine.

These chemical similarities between hallucinogenic compounds and neurohormones with roles in neurophysiology may help to explain hallucinogenic activity and even certain processes of the central nervous system. Other alkaloids—the isoquinolines, tropanes, quinolizidines, and isoxazoles—are more mildly hallucinogenic and may operate differently in the body.

HALLUCINOGENIC ALKALOIDS WITH
THE INDOLE NUCLEUS

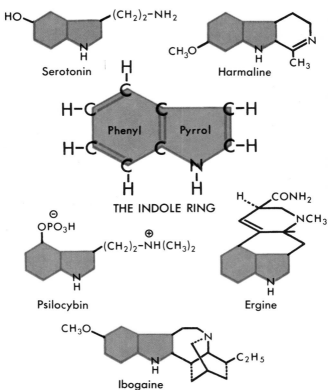

$(CH_2)_2-N(CH_3)_2$

N,N = Dimethyltryptamine

HO— $(CH_2)_2-NH_2$

Serotonin

CH_3O—

CH_3

Harmaline

THE INDOLE RING

Phenyl   Pyrrol

$OPO_3H^{\ominus}$

$(CH_2)_2-NH(CH_3)_2^{\oplus}$

Psilocybin

$CONH_2$

NCH_3

Ergine

CH_3O—

C_2H_5

Ibogaine

PSEUDOHALLUCINOGENS

These are poisonous plant compounds that cause what might be called secondary hallucinations or pseudo-hallucinations. Though not true hallucinogenic agents, they so upset normal body functions that they induce a kind of delirium accompanied by what to all practical purposes are hallucinations. Some components of the essential oils—the aromatic elements responsible for the characteristic odors of plants—appear to act in this way. Components of nutmeg oil are an example. Many plants having such components are extremely dangerous to take internally, especially if ingested in doses high enough to induce hallucinations. Research has not yet shed much light on the kind of psychoactivity produced by such chemicals.

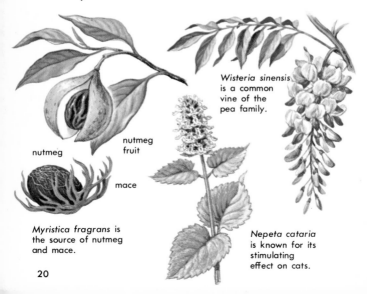

Wisteria sinensis is a common vine of the pea family.

nutmeg

nutmeg fruit

mace

Myristica fragrans is the source of nutmeg and mace.

Nepeta cataria is known for its stimulating effect on cats.

HOW HALLUCINOGENS ARE TAKEN

Hallucinogenic plants are used in a variety of ways, depending on the kind of plant material, on the active chemicals involved, on cultural practices, and on other considerations. Man, in primitive societies everywhere, has shown great ingenuity and perspicacity in bending hallucinogenic plants to his uses.

PLANTS MAY BE EATEN, either fresh or dried, as are peyote and teonanacatl; or juice from the crushed leaves may be drunk, as with *Salvia divinorum* (in Mexico). Occasionally a plant derivative may be eaten, as with hasheesh. More frequently, a beverage may be drunk: ayahuasca, caapi, or yajé from the bark of a vine; the San Pedro cactus; jurema wine; iboga; leaves of toloache; or crushed seeds from the Mexican morning glories. Originally peculiar to New World cultures, where it was one way of using tobacco, smoking is now a widespread method of taking cannabis. Narcotics other than tobacco, such as tupa, may also be smoked.

SNUFFING is a preferred method for using several hallucinogens —yopo, epena, sébil, rapé dos indios. Like smoking, snuffing is a New World custom. A few New World Indians have taken hallucinogens rectally—as in the case of *Anadenanthera*.

One curious method of inducing narcotic effects is the African custom of incising the scalp and rubbing the juice from the onionlike bulb of a species of *Pancratium* across the incisions. This method is a kind of primitive counterpart of the modern hypodermic method.

Several methods may be used in the case of some hallucinogenic plants. *Virola* resin, for example, is licked unchanged, is usually prepared in snuff form, is occasionally made into pellets to be eaten, and may sometimes be smoked.

PLANT ADDITIVES or admixtures to major hallucinogenic species are becoming increasingly important in research. Subsidiary plants are sometimes added to the preparation to alter, increase, or lengthen the narcotic effects of the main ingredients. Thus, in making the ayahuasca, caapi, or yajé drinks, prepared basically from *Banisteriopsis caapi* or *B. inebrians*, several additives are often thrown in: leaves of *Psychotria viridis* or *Banisteriopsis rusbyana*, which themselves contain hallucinogenic tryptamines; or *Brunfelsia* or *Datura*, both of which are hallucinogenic in their own right.

OLD WORLD HALLUCINOGENS

Existing evidence indicates that man in the Old World —Europe, Asia, Africa, and Australia—has made less use of native plants and shrubs for their hallucinogenic properties than has man in the New World.

There is little reason to believe that the vegetation of one half of the globe is poorer or richer in species with hallucinogenic properties than the other half. Why, then, should there be such disparity? Has man in the Old World simply not discovered many of the native hallucinogenic plants? Are some of them too toxic in other ways to be utilized? Or has man in the Old World been culturally less interested in narcotics? We have no real answer. But we do know that the Old World has fewer known species employed hallucinogenically than does the New World: compared with only 15 or 20 species used in the Eastern Hemisphere, the species used hallucinogenically in the Western Hemisphere number more than 100!

Yet some of the Old World hallucinogens today hold places of primacy throughout the world. Cannabis, undoubtedly the most widespread of all the hallucinogens, is perhaps the best example. The several solanaceous ingredients of medieval witches' brews—henbane, nightshade, belladonna, and mandrake—greatly influenced European philosophy, medicine, and even history for many years. Some played an extraordinarily vital religious role in the early Aryan cultures of northern India.

The role of hallucinogens in the cultural and social development of many areas of the Old World is only now being investigated. At every turn, its extent and depth are becoming more evident. But much more needs to be done in the study of hallucinogens and their uses in the Eastern Hemisphere.

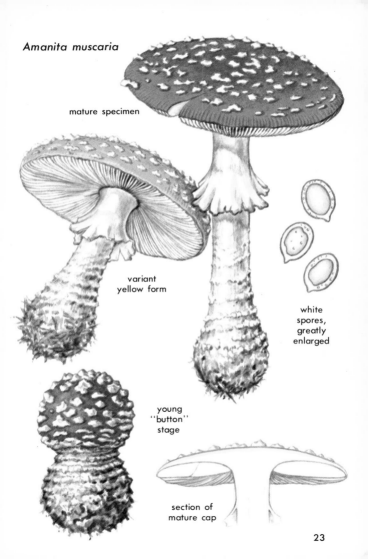

Amanita muscaria

mature specimen

variant
yellow form

white
spores,
greatly
enlarged

young
"button"
stage

section of
mature cap

23

FLY AGARIC MUSHROOM, *Amanita muscaria,* may be one of man's oldest hallucinogens. It has been suggested that perhaps its strange effects contributed to man's early ideas of deity.

Fly agaric mushrooms grow in the north temperate regions of both hemispheres. The Eurasian type has a beautiful deep orange to blood-red cap flecked with white scales. The cap of the usual North American type varies from cream to an orange-yellow. There are also chemical differences between the two, for the New World type is devoid of the strongly hallucinogenic effects of its Old World counterpart.

The use of this mushroom as an orgiastic and shamanistic inebriant was discovered in Siberia in 1730. Subsequently, its utilization has been noted among several isolated groups of Finno-Ugrian peoples (Ostyak and Vogul) in western Siberia and three primitive tribes (Chuckchee, Koryak, and Kamchadal) in northeastern Siberia. These tribes had no other intoxicant until they learned recently of alcohol.

These Siberians ingest the mushroom alone, either sun-dried or toasted slowly over a fire, or they may take it in reindeer milk or with the juice of wild plants, such as a species

Amanita muscaria typically occurs in association with birches.

A Siberian Chukchee man with wooden urine vessel, about to recycle and extend intoxication from *Amanita muscaria*.

of *Vaccinium* and a species of *Epilobium*. When eaten alone, the dried mushrooms are moistened in the mouth and swallowed, or the women may moisten and roll them into pellets for the men to swallow.

A very old and curious practice of these tribesmen is the ritualistic drinking of urine from men who have become intoxicated with the mushroom. The active principles pass through the body and are excreted unchanged or as still active derivatives. Consequently, a few mushrooms may inebriate many people.

The nature of the intoxication varies, but one or several mushrooms induce a condition marked usually by twitching, trembling, slight convulsions, numbness of the limbs, and a feeling of ease characterized by happiness, a desire to sing and dance, colored visions, and macropsia (seeing things greatly enlarged). Violence giving way to a deep sleep may occasionally occur. Participants are sometimes overtaken by curious beliefs, such as that experienced by an ancient tribesman who insisted that he had just been born! Religious fervor often accompanies the inebriation.

Recent studies suggest that this mushroom was the mysterious God-narcotic soma of ancient India. Thousands of years ago, Aryan conquerors, who swept across India, worshiped soma, drinking it in religious ceremonies. Many hymns in the Indian Rig-Veda are devoted to soma and describe the plant and its effects.

The use of soma eventually died out, and its identity has been an enigma for 2,000 years. During the past century, more than 100 plants have been suggested, but none answers the descriptions found in the many hymns. Recent ethnobotanical detective work, leading to its identification as *A. muscaria,* is strengthened by the reference in the vedas to ceremonial urine drinking, since the main intoxicating constituent, muscimole (known

Ibotenic Acid

$$\xrightarrow[\;-H_2O\;]{-CO_2}$$

Muscimole

$\downarrow h\nu$

Muscazone

Chemical formulas of the important *Amanita muscaria* alkaloids.

only in this mushroom), is the sole natural hallucinogenic chemical excreted unchanged from the body.

Only in the last few years, too, has the chemistry of the intoxicating principle been known. For a century, it was believed to be muscarine, but muscarine is present in such minute concentrations that it cannot act as the inebriant. It is now recognized that, in the drying or extraction of the mushrooms, ibotenic acid forms several derivatives. One of these is muscimole, the main pharmacologically active principle. Other compounds, such as muscazone, are found in lesser concentrations and may contribute to the intoxication.

Fly agaric mushroom is so called because of its age-old use in Europe as a fly killer. The mushrooms were left in an open dish. Flies attracted to and settling on them were stunned, succumbing to the insecticidal properties of the plant.

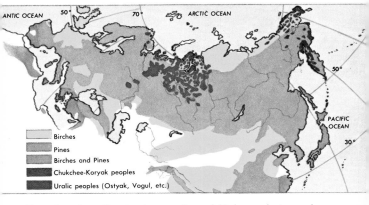

Map of northern Eurasia shows regions of birches and pines, where *Amanita muscaria* typically grows, and areas inhabited by ethnic groups that use the mushroom as an hallucinogen.

AGARA (*Galbulimima belgraveana*) is a tall forest tree of Malaysia and Australia. In Papua, natives make a drink by boiling the leaves and bark with the leaves of ereriba. When they imbibe it, they become violently intoxicated, eventually falling into a deep sleep during which they experience visions and fantastic dreams. Some 28 alkaloids have been isolated from this tree, and although they are biologically active, the psychoactive principle is still unknown. Agara is one of four species of *Galbulimima* and belongs to the Himantandraceae, a rare family related to the magnolias.

ERERIBA, an undetermined species of *Homalomena,* is a stout herb reported to have narcotic effects when its leaves are taken with the leaves and bark of agara. The active chemical constituent is unknown. Ereriba is a member of the aroid family, Araceae. There are some 140 species of *Homalomena* native to tropical Asia and South America.

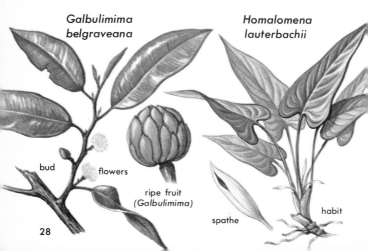

Galbulimima
belgraveana

Homalomena
lauterbachii

bud

flowers

ripe fruit
(*Galbulimima*)

spathe

habit

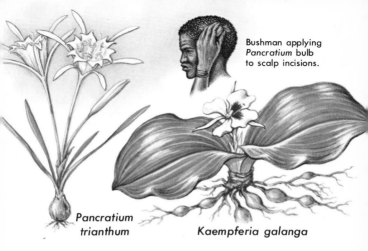

Bushman applying *Pancratium* bulb to scalp incisions.

Pancratium trianthum   *Kaempferia galanga*

KWASHI (*Pancratium trianthum*) is considered to be psychoactive by the Bushmen in Dobe, Botswana. The bulb of this perennial is reputedly rubbed over incisions in the head to induce visual hallucinations. Nothing is known of its chemical constitution. Of the 14 other species of *Pancratium*, mainly of Asia and Africa, many are known to contain psychoactive principles, mostly alkaloids. Some species are potent cardiac poisons. *Pancratium* belongs to the amaryllis family, Amaryllidaceae.

GALANGA or MARABA (*Kaempferia galanga*) is an herb rich in essential oils. Natives in New Guinea eat the rhizome of the plant as an hallucinogen. It is valued locally as a condiment and, like others of the 70 species in the genus, it is used in local folk medicine to bring boils to a head and to hasten the healing of burns and wounds. It is a member of the ginger family, Zingiberaceae. Phytochemical studies have revealed no psychoactive principle.

Hemp field in Afghanistan, showing partly harvested crop of the short, conical *Cannabis indica* grown there.

MARIHUANA, HASHEESH, or HEMP (species of the genus *Cannabis*), also called Kif, Bhang, or Charas, is one of the oldest cultivated plants. It is also one of the most widely spread weeds, having escaped cultivation, appearing as an adventitious plant everywhere, except in the polar regions and the wet, forested tropics.

Cannabis is the source of hemp fiber, an edible fruit, an industrial oil, a medicine, and a narcotic. Despite its great age and its economic importance, the plant is still poorly understood, characterized more by what we do not know about it than by what we know.

Cannabis is a rank, weedy annual that is extremely variable and may attain a height of 18 feet. Flourishing best in disturbed, nitrogen-rich soils near human habitations, it has been called a "camp follower," going with man into new areas.

It is normally dioecious—that is, the male and female parts are on different plants. The male or staminate plant is usually weaker than the female or pistillate plant. Pistillate flowers grow in the leaf axils. The intoxicating constituents are normally concentrated in a resin in the developing female flowers and adjacent leaves and stems.

CLASSIFICATION OF CANNABIS is disputed by botanists. They disagree about the family to which it belongs and also about the number of species. The plant is sometimes placed in the fig or mulberry family (Moraceae) or the nettle family (Urticaceae), but it is now usually separated, together with the hop plant (*Humulus*), into a distinct family: Cannabaceae.

It has been widely thought that there is one species, *Cannabis sativa*, which, partly as a result of selection by man, has developed many "races" or "varieties," for better fiber, for more oil content, or for stronger narcotic content. Selection for narcotic activity has been especially notable in such areas as India, where intoxicating properties have had religious significance. Environment also has probably influenced this biologically changeable species, especially for fiber excellence and narcotic activity. Current research indicates that there may be other species: *C. indica* and *C. ruderalis*. All *Cannabis* is native to central Asia.

Cannabis leaves are palmately divided—normally into 3–7 leaflets, occasionally into 11–13. Leaflets vary in length from 2 to 6 inches.

MARIHUANA
Cannabis sativa

male buds
and flower,
enlarged

top of male
plant, in flower

seedling

stamen, greatly
enlarged, shedding
pollen

habit of
male plant

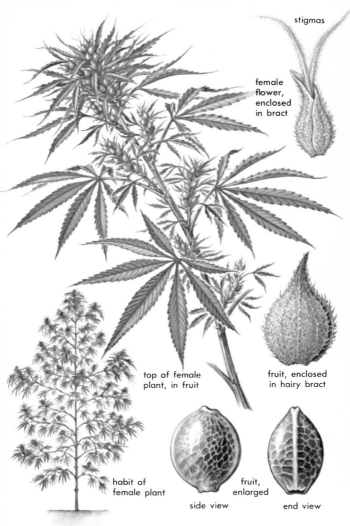

stigmas

female flower, enclosed in bract

top of female plant, in fruit

fruit, enclosed in hairy bract

habit of female plant

fruit, enlarged

side view

end view

33

Chinese characters TA MA, the oldest known name for cannabis.

大 = TA (pronounced DA). Literally this means an adult man, and by extension may signify great or tall.

麻 = MA. It represents a fiber plant, literally a clump of plants (林), growing near a dwelling (广). Hence, the two symbols together mean "the tall fiber plant," which everywhere in China signifies cannabis.

HISTORY OF CANNABIS USE dates to ancient times. Hemp fabrics from the late 8th century B.C. have been found in Turkey. Specimens have turned up in an Egyptian site nearly 4,000 years of age. In ancient Thebes, the plant was made into a drink with opium-like effects. The Scythians, who threw cannabis seeds and leaves on hot stones in steam baths to produce an intoxicating smoke, grew the plant along the Volga 3,000 years ago.

Chinese tradition puts the use of the plant back 4,800 years. Indian medical writing, compiled before 1000 B.C., reports therapeutic uses of cannabis. That the early Hindus appreciated its intoxicating properties is attested by such names as "heavenly guide" and "soother of grief." The Chinese referred to cannabis as "liberator of sin" and "delight giver." The Greek physician Galen wrote, about A.D. 160, that general use of hemp in cakes produced narcotic effects. In 13th-century Asia Minor, organized murderers, rewarded with hasheesh, were known as hashishins, from which may come the term assassin in European languages.

Hemp as a source of fiber was introduced by the Pilgrims to New England and by the Spanish and Portuguese to their colonies in the New World.

18"

Objects connected with the use of cannabis were found in frozen tombs of the ancient Scythians, in the Altai Mountains on the border between Russia and Outer Mongolia.

The small, tepee-like structure was covered with a felt or leather mat and stood over the copper censer (four-legged stool-like object). Carbonized hemp seeds were found nearby. The two-handled pot contained cannabis fruits. The Scythian custom of breathing cannabis fumes in the steam bath was mentioned about 500 B.C. by the Greek naturalist Herodotus.

THE MEDICINAL VALUE OF CANNABIS has been known for centuries. Its long history of use in folk medicine is significant, and it has been included more recently in Western pharmacopoeias. It was listed in the United States *Pharmacopoeia* until the 1930's as valuable, especially in the treatment of hysteria. The progress made in modern research encourages the belief that so prolific a chemical factory as *Cannabis* may indeed offer potential for new medicines.

THE CHEMISTRY OF CANNABIS is complex. Many organic compounds have been isolated, some with narcotic properties and others without. A fresh plant yields mainly cannabidiolic acids, precursors of the tetrahydrocannabinols and related constituents, such as cannabinol, cannabidiol, tetrahydrocannabinol-carboxylic acid, stereoisomers of tetrahydrocannabinol, and cannabichromene.

It has been demonstrated recently that the main effects are attributable to delta-1-tetrahydrocannabinol. The tetrahydrocannabinols, which form an oily mixture of several isomers, are non-nitrogenous organic compounds derived from terpenes (see page 16). They are not alkaloids, although traces of alkaloids have been reported in the plant.

Until recently, little was known about the effects of pure tetrahydrocannabinol on man. Controlled studies are basic to any progress. These are now possible with the recent synthesis of the compound, a major advance in studying the mechanism of physiological activity of this intoxicant. Because the crude cannabis preparations normally used as a narcotic vary greatly in their chemical composition, any correlations of their biological activity would be relatively meaningless.

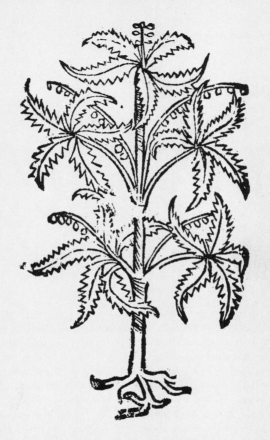

Caput. lxxxvj.

A crude woodcut illustration of cannabis from the 1517 edition of the European herbal *Ortus sanitatis de herbis et plantis.*

three contemporary designs

Bantu traveler's dagga pipe (Africa)

copper water pipe from Afghanistan

Moroccan hasheesh pipe

African bhang pipe

silver hookah from India

Bushman animal-horn pipe

Assortment of cannabis pipes and water pipes.

METHODS OF USING CANNABIS vary. In the New World, marihuana (maconha in Brazil) is smoked—the dried, crushed flowering tips or leaves, often mixed with tobacco in cigarettes, or "reefers." Hasheesh, the resin from the female plant, is eaten or smoked, often in water pipes, by millions in Moslem countries of northern Africa and western Asia. In Afghanistan and Pakistan, the resin is commonly smoked. Asiatic Indians regularly employ three preparations narcotically: bhang consists of plants that are gathered green, dried, and made into a drink with water or milk or into a candy (majun) with sugar and spices; charas, normally smoked or eaten with spices, is pure resin; ganjah, usually smoked with tobacco, consists of resin-rich dried tops from the female plant. Many of these unusually potent preparations may be derived from C. *indica*.

NARCOTIC USE OF CANNABIS has grown in popularity in the past 40 years as the plant has spread to nearly all parts of the globe. The narcotic use of cannabis in the United States dates from the 1920's and seems to have started in New Orleans and vicinity. Increase in the plant's use as an inebriant in Western countries, especially in urban centers, has led to major problems and dilemmas for European and American authorities. There is a sharp division of opinion as to whether the widespread narcotic use of cannabis is a vice that must be stamped out or is an innocuous habit that should be permitted legally. The subject is debated hotly, usually with limited knowledge. We do not yet have the medical, social, legal, and moral information on which to base a sound judgment. As one writer has said, the marihuana problem needs "more light and less heat." Controlled, scientifically valid experiments with cannabis, involving large numbers of individuals, have not as yet been made.

Contemporary American cannabis shoulder patches.

EFFECTS OF CANNABIS, even more than of other hallucinogens, are highly variable from person to person and from one plant strain to another. This variability comes mainly from the unstable character of some of the constituents. Over a period of time, for example, the inactive cannabidiolic acid converts to active tetrahydrocannabinols and eventually to inactive cannabinol, such chemical changes usually taking place more rapidly in tropical than in cooler climates. Material from plants of different ages may thus vary in narcotic effect.

The principal narcotic effect is euphoria. The plant is sometimes not classified as hallucinogenic, and it is true that its characteristics are not typically psychotomimetic. Everything from a mild sense of ease and well-being to fantastic dreams and visual and auditory hallucinations are reported. Beautiful sights, wonderful music, and aberrations of sound often entrance the mind; bizarre adventures to fill a century take place in a matter of minutes.

Soon after taking the drug, a subject may find himself in a dreamy state of altered consciousness. Normal thought is interrupted, and ideas are sometimes plenti-

In many parts of Asia the use of cannabis preparations is both socially and legally acceptable. In predominantly Moslem countries, cannabis is usually smoked in water pipes, sometimes called hookahs. The illustration shows an Afghani using one of the many kinds of water pipes seen in Asia.

Market forms of cannabis include finely ground or "manicured" marihuana, "reefers" (smaller than commercial tobacco cigarettes), pure hasheesh, and compressed kilo bricks.

ful, though confused. A feeling of exaltation and inner joy may alternate, even dangerously, with feelings of depression, moodiness, uncontrollable fear of death, and panic. Perception of time is almost invariably altered. An exaggeration of sound, out of all relation to the real force of the sound emitted, may be accompanied by a curiously hypnotic sense of rhythm. Although the occasional vivid visual hallucinations may have sexual coloring, the often-reported aphrodisiac properties of the drug have not been substantiated.

Whether cannabis should be classified primarily as a stimulant or depressant or both has never been determined. The drug's activities beyond the central nervous system seem to be secondary. They consist of a rise in pulse rate and blood pressure, tremor, vertigo, difficulty in muscular coordination, increased tactile sensitivity, and dilation of the pupils.

Although cannabis is definitely not addictive, psychological dependence may often result from continual use of the drug.

TURKESTAN MINT *(Lagochilus inebrians)* is a small shrub of the dry steppes of Turkestan. For centuries it has been the source of an intoxicant among the Tajik, Tartar, Turkoman, and Uzbek tribesmen. The leaves, gathered in October, are toasted, sometimes mixed with stems, fruits, and flowers. Drying and storage increase their aromatic fragrance. Honey and sugar are often added to reduce their intense bitterness.

Valued as a folk medicine and included in the 8th edition of the Russian pharmacopoeia, it is used to treat skin disease, to help check hemorrhages, and to provide sedation for nervous disorders. A crystalline compound isolated from the plant and named lagochiline has proved to be aditerpene. Whether or not it produces the psychoactive effects of the whole plant is unknown. There are some 34 other species of *Lagochilus*. Members of the mint family, Labiatae, they are native from central Asia to Iran and Afghanistan.

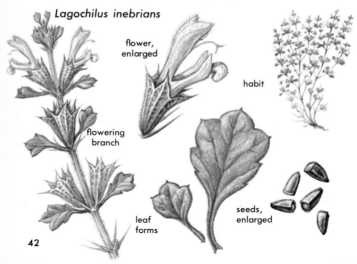

Lagochilus inebrians

flower, enlarged

habit

flowering branch

leaf forms

seeds, enlarged

42

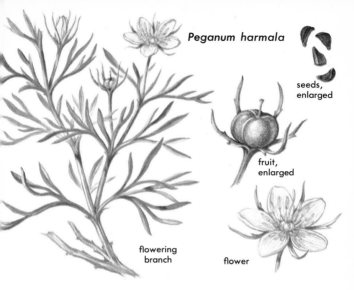

Peganum harmala

seeds, enlarged

fruit, enlarged

flowering branch

flower

SYRIAN RUE (*Peganum harmala*) grows from the Mediterranean to northern India, Mongolia, and Manchuria. Everywhere it has many uses in folk medicine. Its seeds have been employed as a spice, and its fruits are the source of a red dye and an oil.

The seeds possess known hallucinogenic alkaloids, especially harmine and harmaline. The esteem in which the peoples of Asia hold the plant is so extraordinary that it might indicate a former religious use as an hallucinogen, but the purposeful use of the plant to induce visions has not yet been established through the literature or field work.

The caltrop family, Zygophyllaceae, to which Syrian rue belongs, comprises about two dozen genera native to dry parts of the tropics and subtropics of both hemispheres.

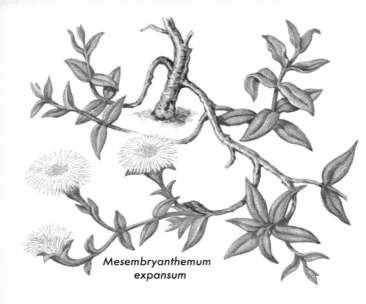

Mesembryanthemum
expansum

KANNA (*Mesembryanthemum expansum* and *M. tortuosum*) is the common name of two species of South African plants. There is strong evidence that one or both were used by the Hottentots of southern Africa as vision-inducing narcotics. More than two centuries ago, it was reported that the Hottentots chewed the root of kanna, or channa, keeping the chewed material in the mouth, with these results: "Their animal spirits were awakened, their eyes sparkled and their faces manifested laughter and gaiety. Thousands of delightsome ideas appeared, and a pleasant jollity which enabled them to be amused by simple jests. By taking the substance to excess, they lost consciousness and fell into a terrible delirium."

Since the narcotic use of these two species has not been observed directly, various botanists have suggested

Mesembryanthemum tortuosum

root detail

that the hallucinogenic kanna may actually have been cannabis or other intoxicating plants, such as several species of *Sclerocarya* of the cashew family. These two species of *Mesembryanthemum* do have the common name kanna, however, and they also contain alkaloids that have sedative, cocainelike properties capable of producing torpor in man.

In the drier parts of South Africa, there are altogether 1,000 species of *Mesembryanthemum*—many, like the ice plant, of bizarre form. About two dozen species, including the two described here, are considered by some botanists to represent a separate genus, *Sceletium*. All belong to the carpetweed family, Aizoaceae, mainly South African, and are believed to be related to the pokeweed, pink, and cactus families.

BELLADONNA *(Atropa belladonna)* is well known as a highly poisonous species capable of inducing various kinds of hallucinations. It entered into the folklore and mythology of virtually all European peoples, who feared its deadly power. It was one of the ingredients of the truly hallucinogenic brews and ointments concocted by the so-called witches of medieval Europe. The attractive shiny berries of the plant still often cause it to be accidentally eaten, with resultant poisoning.

The name belladonna ("beautiful lady" in Italian) comes from a curious custom practiced by Italian women of high society during medieval times. They would drop the sap of the plant into the eye to dilate the pupil enormously, inducing a kind of drunken or glassy stare, considered in that period to enhance feminine beauty and sensuality.

The main active principle in belladonna is the alkaloid hyoscyamine, but the more psychoactive scopolamine is also present. Atropine has also been found, but whether it is present in the living plant or is formed during extraction is not clear. Belladonna is a commercial source of atropine, an alkaloid with a wide variety of uses in modern medicine, especially as an antispasmodic, an antisecretory, and as a mydriatic and cardiac stimulant. The alkaloids occur throughout the plant but are concentrated especially in the leaves and roots.

There are four species of *Atropa* distributed in Europe and from central Asia to the Himalayas. *Atropa* belongs to the nightshade family, Solanaceae. Belladonna is native to Europe and Asia Minor. Until the 19th century, commercial collection was primarily from wild sources, but since that time cultivation has been initiated in the United States, Europe, and India, where it is an important source of medicinal drugs.

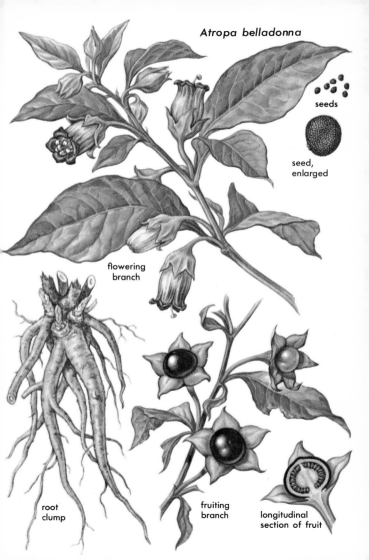

Atropa belladonna

seeds

seed,
enlarged

flowering
branch

root
clump

fruiting
branch

longitudinal
section of fruit

HENBANE (*Hyoscyamus niger*) was often included in the witches' brews and other toxic preparations of medieval Europe to cause visual hallucinations and the sensation of flight. An annual or biennial native to Europe, it has long been valued in medicine as a sedative and an anodyne to induce sleep.

The principal alkaloid of henbane is hyoscyamine, but the more hallucinogenic scopolamine is also present in significant amounts, along with several other alkaloids in smaller concentrations.

Henbane is one of 20 species of *Hyoscyamus*, members of the nightshade family, Solanaceae. They are native to Europe, northern Africa, and western and central Asia.

Medieval witches cooking "magic" brew with toad and henbane.

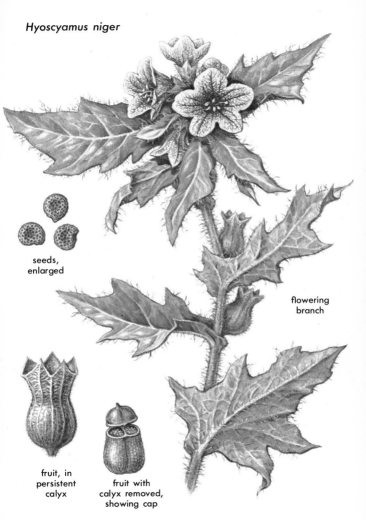

Hyoscyamus niger

seeds,
enlarged

flowering
branch

fruit, in
persistent
calyx

fruit with
calyx removed,
showing cap

49

MANDRAKE (*Mandragora officinarum*), an hallucinogen with a fantastic history, has long been known and feared for its toxicity. Its complex history as a magic hypnotic in the folklore of Europe cannot be equaled by any species anywhere. Mandrake was a panacea. Its folk uses in medieval Europe were inextricably bound up with the "Doctrine of Signatures," an old theory holding that the appearance of an object indicates its special properties. The root of mandrake was likened to the form of a man or woman; hence its magic. If a mandrake were pulled from the earth, according to superstition, its unearthly shrieks could drive its collector

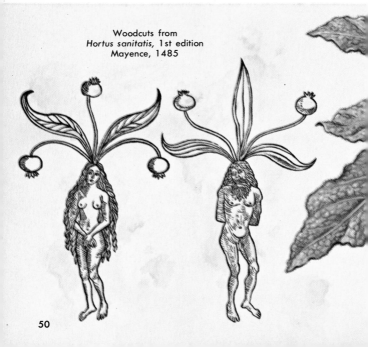

Woodcuts from
Hortus sanitatis, 1st edition
Mayence, 1485

mad. In many regions, the people claimed strong aphrodisiac properties for mandrake. The superstitious hold of this plant in Europe persisted for centuries.

Mandrake, with the tropane alkaloids hyoscyamine, scopolamine, and others, was an active hallucinogenic ingredient of many of the witches' brews of Europe. In fact, it was undoubtedly one of the most potent ingredients in those complex preparations.

Mandrake and five other species of *Mandragora* belong to the nightshade family, Solanaceae, and are native to the area between the Mediterranean and the Himalayas.

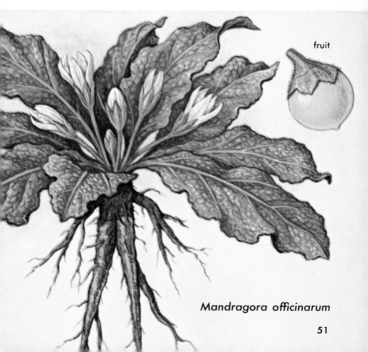

fruit

Mandragora officinarum

DHATURA and DUTRA (*Datura metel*) are the common names in India for an important Old World species of *Datura*. The narcotic properties of this purple-flowered member of the deadly nightshade family, Solanaceae, have been known and valued in India since prehistory. The plant has a long history in other countries as well. Some writers have credited it with being responsible for the intoxicating smoke associated with the Oracle of Delphi. Early Chinese writings report an hallucinogen that has been identified with this species. And it is undoubtedly the plant that Avicenna, the Arabian physician, mentioned under the name jouzmathel in the 11th century. Its use as an aphrodisiac in the East Indies was recorded in 1578. The plant was held sacred in China, where people believed that when Buddha preached, heaven sprinkled the plant with dew.

Nevertheless, the utilization of *Datura* preparations in Asia entailed much less ritual than in the New World. In many parts of Asia, even today, seeds of *Datura* are often mixed with food and tobacco for illicit use, especially by thieves for stupefying victims, who may remain seriously intoxicated for several days.

Datura metel is commonly mixed with cannabis and smoked in Asia to this day. Leaves of a white-flowered form of the plant (considered by some botanists to be a distinct species, *D. fastuosa*) are smoked with cannabis or tobacco in many parts of Africa and Asia.

The plant contains highly toxic alkaloids, the principal one being scopolamine. This hallucinogen is present in heaviest concentrations in the leaves and seeds. Scopolamine is found also in the New World species of *Datura* (pp. 142–147). *Datura ferox,* a related Old World species, not so widespread in Asia, is also valued for its narcotic and medicinal properties.

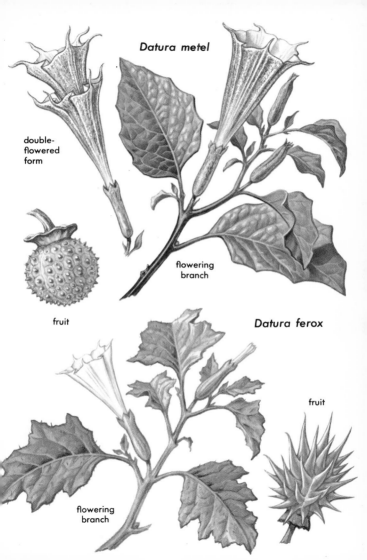

Datura metel

double-flowered form

fruit

flowering branch

Datura ferox

fruit

flowering branch

IBOGA *(Tabernanthe iboga)*, native to Gabon and the Congo, is the only member of the dogbane family, Apocynaceae, known to be used as an hallucinogen. The plant is of growing importance, providing the strongest single force against the spread of Christianity and Islam in this region.

The yellowish root of the iboga plant is employed in the initiation rites of a number of secret societies, the most famous being the Bwiti cult. Entrance into the cult is conditional on having "seen" the god plant Bwiti, which is accomplished through the use of iboga.

The drug, discovered by Europeans toward the middle of the last century, has a reputation as a powerful stimulant and aphrodisiac. Hunters use it to keep themselves awake all night. Large doses induce unworldly visions, and "sorcerers" often take the drug to seek information from ancestors and the spirit world.

Ibogaine is the principal indole alkaloid among a dozen

others found in iboga. The pharmacology of ibogaine is well known. In addition to being an hallucinogen, **ibogaine** in large doses is a strong central nervous system stimulant, leading to convulsions, paralysis, and arrest of respiration.

"Payment of the Ancestors," taking place between two shrubby bushes of *Tabernanthe iboga* in the Fang Cult of Bwiti, Congo. (Photo by J. W. Fernandez.)

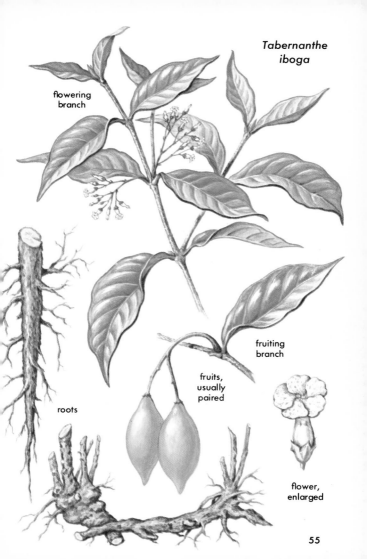

Tabernanthe iboga

flowering branch

fruiting branch

fruits, usually paired

roots

flower, enlarged

55

NEW WORLD HALLUCINOGENS

In the New World—North, Central, and South America and the West Indies—the number and cultural importance of hallucinogens reached amazing heights in the past—and in places their role is undiminished.

More than ninety species are employed for their intoxicating principles, compared to fewer than a dozen in the Old World. It would not be an exaggeration to say that some of the New World cultures, particularly in Mexico and South America, were practically enslaved by the religious use of hallucinogens, which acquired a deep and controlling significance in almost every aspect of life. Cultures in North America and the West Indies used fewer hallucinogens, and their role often seemed secondary. Although tobacco and coca, the source of cocaine, have become of worldwide importance, none of the true hallucinogens of the Western Hemisphere has assumed the global significance of the Old World cannabis.

No ethnological study of American Indians can be considered complete without an in-depth appreciation of their hallucinogens. Unexpected discoveries have come from studying the hallucinogenic use of New World plants. Many hallucinogenic preparations called for the addition of plant additives capable of altering the intoxication. The accomplishments of aboriginal Americans in the use of mixtures have been extraordinary.

While known New World hallucinogens are numerous, studies are still uncovering species new to the list. The most curious aspect of the studies, however, is why, in view of their vital importance to New World cultures, the botanical identities of many of the hallucinogens remained unknown until comparatively recent times.

PUFFBALLS (*Lycoperdon mixtecorum* and *L. marginatum*) are used by the Mixtec Indians of Oaxaca, Mexico, as auditory hallucinogens. After eating these fungi, a native hears voices and echoes. There is apparently no ceremony connected with puffballs, and they do not enjoy the place as divinatory agents that the mushrooms do in Oaxaca. *L. mixtecorum* is the stronger of the two. It is called gi-i-wa, meaning "fungus of the first quality." *L. marginatum*, which has a strong odor of excrement, is known as gi-i-sa-wa, meaning "fungus of the second quality."

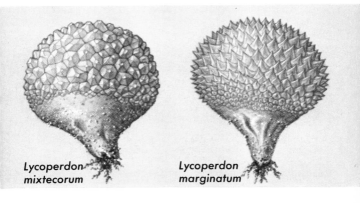

Lycoperdon mixtecorum

Lycoperdon marginatum

Although intoxicating substances have not yet been found in the puffballs, there are reports in the literature that some of them have had narcotic effects when eaten. Most of the estimated 50 to 100 species of *Lycoperdon* grow in mossy forests of the temperate zone. They belong to the Lycoperdaceae, a family of the Gasteromycetes.

The use of hallucinogenic mushrooms, which dates back several thousand years, centers in the mountains of southern Mexico.

MUSHROOMS of many species were used as hallucinogens by the Aztec Indians, who called them teonanacatl, meaning "flesh of the gods" in the Nahuatl Indian language. These mushrooms, all of the family Agaricaceae, are still valued in Mexican magico-religious rites. They belong to four genera: *Conocybe* and *Panaeolus,* almost cosmopolitan in their range; *Psilocybe,* found in North and South America, Europe, and Asia; and *Stropharia,* known in North America, the West Indies, and Europe.

MUSHROOM WORSHIP seems to have roots in centuries of native tradition. Mexican frescoes, going back to A.D. 300, have designs suggestive of mushrooms. Even more remarkable are the artifacts called mushroom stones (p. 60), excavated in large numbers from highland Maya sites in Guatemala and dating back to 1000 B.C. Consisting of a stem with a human or animal face and surmounted by an umbrella-shaped top, they long puzzled archaeologists. Now interpreted as a kind of icon connected with religious rituals, they indicate that 3,000 years ago, a sophisticated religion surrounded the sacramental use of these fungi.

It has been suggested that perhaps mushrooms were the earliest hallucinogenic plants to be discovered. The other-worldly experience induced by these mysterious forms of plant life could easily have suggested a spiritual plane of existence.

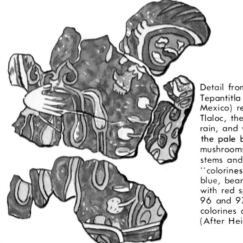

Detail from a fresco at Tepantitla (Teotihuacán, Mexico) representing Tlaloc, the god of clouds, rain, and waters. Note the pale blue mushrooms with orange stems and also the "colorines"—the darker blue, bean-shaped forms with red spots. See pages 96 and 97 for discussion of colorines and piule. (After Heim and Wasson.)

MUSHROOM STONES

Typical icons probably associated with mushroom cults dating back 3,000 years in Guatemala.

EARLY USE OF THE SACRED MUSHROOMS is known mainly from the extensive descriptions written by the Spanish clerics. For this we owe them a great debt.

One chronicler, writing in the mid-1500's, after the conquest of Mexico, referred frequently to those mushrooms "which are harmful and intoxicate like wine," so that those who eat them "see visions, feel a faintness of heart and are provoked to lust"; the natives "when they begin to get excited by them start dancing, singing, weeping. Some do not want to eat but sit down . . . and see themselves dying in a vision; others see themselves being eaten by a wild beast; others imagine that they are capturing prisoners of war, that they are rich, that they possess many slaves, that they had committed adultery and were to have their heads crushed for the offense. . . ."

A work of Aztec medicine mentions three kinds of intoxicating mushrooms. One, teyhuintli, causes "madness that on occasion is lasting, of which the symptom is an uncontrollable laughter; there are others which . . . bring before the eyes all sorts of things, such as wars and the likeness of demons. Yet others are not less desired by princes for their festivals and banquets, and these fetch a high price. With night-long vigils are they sought, awesome and terrifying."

Detail from fresco at Sacuala, Teotihuacán, Mexico, showing four greenish "mushrooms" that seem to be emerging from the mouth of a god, possibly the Sun God.

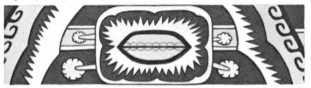

SPANISH OPPOSITION to the Aztecs' worship of pagan deities with the sacramental aid of mushrooms was strong. Although the Spanish conquerors of Mexico hated and attacked the religious use of all hallucinogens —peyote, ololiuqui, toloache, and others—teonanacatl was the target of special wrath. Their religious fanaticism was drawn especially toward this despised and feared form of plant life that, through its vision-giving powers, held the Indian in awe, allowing him to commune directly with his gods. The new religion, Christianity, had nothing so attractive to offer him. Trying to stamp out the use of the mushrooms, the Spaniards succeeded only in driving the custom into the hinterlands, where it persists today. Not only did it persist, but the ritual adopted many Christian aspects, and the modern ritual is a pagan-Christian blend.

The pagan god of the underworld speaks through the mushroom, teonanacatl, as represented by a Mexican artist in the 16th century. (From the *Magliabecchiano Codex*, Biblioteca Nazionale, Florence.)

A 16th-century illustration of teonanacatl (a), the intoxicating mushroom of the Aztecs, still valued in Mexican magico-religious rites; identity of (b) is unknown. From Sahagún's *Historia general de las cosas de Nueva España*, Vol. IV (Florentine Codex).

IDENTIFICATION OF THE SACRED MUSHROOMS was slow in coming. Driven into hiding by the Spaniards, the mushroom cult was not encountered in Mexico for four centuries. During that time, although the Mexican flora was known to include various toxic mushrooms, it was believed that the Aztecs had tried to protect their real sacred plant: they had led the Spaniards to believe that teonanacatl meant mushroom, when it actually meant peyote. It was pointed out that the symptoms of mushroom intoxication coincided remarkably with those described for peyote intoxication and that dried mushrooms might easily have been confused with the shriveled brown heads of the peyote cactus. But the numerous detailed references by careful writers, including medical men trained in botany, argued against this theory.

Not until the 1930's were botanists able to identify specimens of mushrooms found in actual use in divinatory rites in Mexico. Later work has shown that more than 20 species of mushrooms are similarly employed among seven or eight tribes in southern Mexico.

THE MODERN MUSHROOM CEREMONY of the Mazatec Indians of northeastern Oaxaca illustrates the importance of the ritual in present-day Mexico and how the sacred character of these plants has persisted from pre-conquest times. The divine mushrooms are gathered during the new moon on the hillsides before dawn by a virgin; they are often consecrated on the altar of the local Catholic church. Their strange growth pattern helps make mushrooms mysterious and awesome to the Mazatec, who call them 'nti-si-tho, meaning "worshipful object that springs forth." They believe that the mushroom springs up miraculously and that it may be sent from outer realms on thunderbolts. As one Indian put it poetically: "The little mushroom comes of itself, no one knows whence, like the wind that comes we know not when or why."

The all-night Mazatec ceremony, led usually by a woman shaman (curandera), comprises long, complicated, and curiously repetitive chants, percussive beats, and

Curandera with Mazatec patient and dish of sacred mushrooms. Scene is typical of the all-night mushroom ceremony. Curandera is under the influence of the mushrooms.

prayers. Often a curing rite takes place during which the practitioner, through the "power" of the sacred mushrooms, communicates and intercedes with supernatural forces. There is no question of the vibrant relevance of the mushroom rituals to modern Indian life in southern Mexico. None of the attraction of these divine mushrooms has been lost as a result of contact with Christianity or modern ideas. The spirit of reverence characteristic of the mushroom ceremony is as profound as that of any of the world's great religions.

KINDS OF MUSHROOMS USED by different shamans are determined partly by personal preference and partly by the purpose of the use. Seasonal and regional availability also have a bearing on the choice. *Stropharia cubensis* and *Psilocybe mexicana* may be the most commonly employed, but half a dozen other species of *Psilocybe* as well as *Conocybe siliginoides* and *Panaeolus sphinctrinus* are also important. The native names are colorful and sometimes significant. *Psilocybe aztecorum* is called "children of the waters"; *P. zapotecorum,* "crown-of-thorns mushroom"; and *P. caerulescens* var. *nigripes,* "mushroom of superior reason." (See illustrations on pp. 66–67). The possibility exists that other hallucinogenic species of mushrooms are also used.

It is possible, too, that *Psilocybe* species are used as inebriants outside of Mexico. *P. yungensis* has been suggested as the mysterious "tree mushroom" that early Jesuit missionaries reported as being employed by the Yurimagua Indians of Amazonian Peru as the source of a potent intoxicating beverage. This species is known to contain an hallucinogenic principle. Field work in modern times, however, has not disclosed the narcotic use of any mushrooms in the Amazon area.

HALLUCINOGENIC
MUSHROOMS

*Psilocybe
semperviva*

*Psilocybe caerulescens
var. mazatecorum*

Psilocybe aztecorum

Psilocybe yungensis

*Psilocybe
mexicana*

*Psilocybe
caerulescens
var. nigripes*

*Psilocybe
zapotecorum*

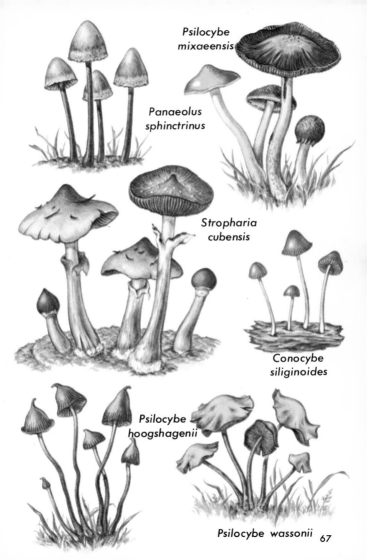

Psilocybe mixaeensis

Panaeolus sphinctrinus

Stropharia cubensis

Conocybe siliginoides

Psilocybe hoogshagenii

Psilocybe wassonii

67

THE EFFECTS OF THE MUSHROOMS include muscular relaxation or limpness, pupil enlargement, hilarity, and difficulty in concentration. The mushrooms cause both visual and auditory hallucinations. Visions are breathtakingly lifelike, in color, and in constant motion. They are followed by lassitude, mental and physical depression, and alteration of time and space perception. The user seems to be isolated from the world around him; without loss of consciousness, he becomes wholly indifferent to his surroundings, and his dreamlike state becomes reality to him. This peculiarity of the intoxication makes it interesting to psychiatrists.

One investigator who ate mushrooms in a Mexican Indian ceremony wrote that "your body lies in the darkness, heavy as lead, but your spirit seems to soar . . . and with the speed of thought to travel where it listeth, in time and space, accompanied by the shaman's singing . . . What you are seeing and . . . hearing appear as one; the music assumes harmonious shapes, giving visual form to its harmonies, and what you are seeing takes on the modalities of music—the music of the spheres.

"All your senses are similarly affected; the cigarette . . . smells as no cigarette before had ever smelled; the glass of simple water is infinitely better than champagne . . . the bemushroomed person is poised in space, a disembodied eye, invisible, incorporeal, seeing but not seen . . . he is the five senses disembodied . . . your soul is free, loses all sense of time, alert as it never was before, living an eternity in a night, seeing infinity in a grain of sand . . . [The visions may be of] almost anything . . . except the scenes of your everyday life." As with other hallucinogens, the effects of the mushrooms may vary with mood and setting.

A scientist's description of his experience after eating 32 dried specimens of *Psilocybe mexicana* was as follows: ". . . When the doctor supervising the experiment bent over me . . . he was transformed into an Aztec priest, and I would not have been astonished if he had drawn an obsidian knife . . . it amused me to see how the Germanic face . . . had acquired a purely Indian expression. At the peak of the intoxication . . . the rush of interior pictures, mostly abstract motifs rapidly changing in shape and color, reached such an alarming degree that I feared that I would be torn into this whirlpool of form and color and would dissolve. After about six hours, the dream came to an end . . . I felt my return to everyday reality to be a happy return from a strange, fantastic but quite really experienced world into an old and familiar home."

CHEMICAL CONSTITUTION of the hallucinogenic mushrooms has surprised scientists. A white crystalline tryptamine of unusual structure—an acidic phosphoric acid ester of 4-hydroxydimethyltryptamine—was isolated. This indole derivative, named psilocybin, is a new type of structure, a 4-substituted tryptamine with a phosphoric acid radical, a type never before known as a naturally occurring constituent of plant tissue. Some of the mushrooms also contain minute amounts of another indolic compound—psilocin—which is unstable. While psilocybin has been found also in European and North American mushrooms, apparently only in Mexico and Guatemala have psilocybin-containing mushrooms been purposefully used for ceremonial intoxication.

Psilocin is believed by some biochemists to be the precursor of the more stable psilocybin.

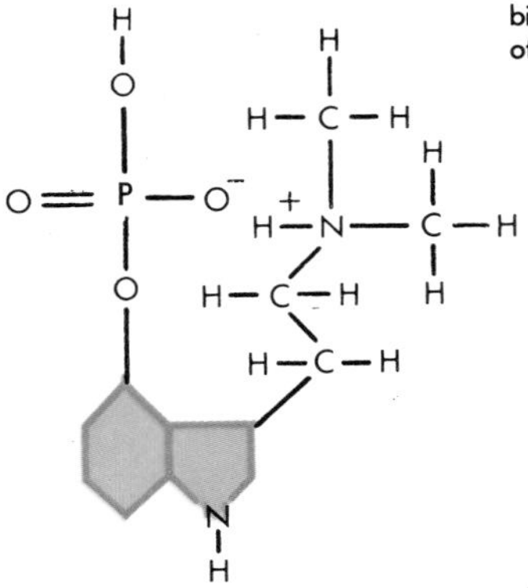

Psilocybin

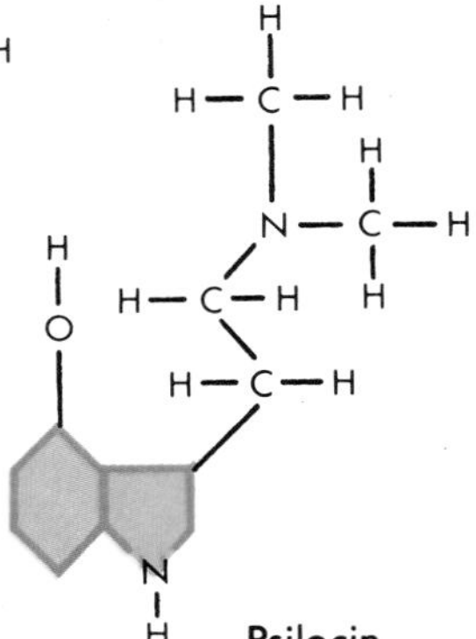

Psilocin

A laboratory culture of *Psilocybe mexicana*, grown from spores, an innovation that speeded analysis of the ephemeral mushroom. (After Heim & Wasson: *Les Champignons Hallucinogènes du Mexique*)

CHEMICAL INVESTIGATION of the Mexican mushrooms was difficult until they could be cultivated. They are almost wholly water and great quantities of them are needed for chemical analyses because their chemical constitution is so ephemeral. The clarification of the chemistry of the Mexican mushrooms was possible only because mycologists were able to cultivate the plants in numbers sufficient to satisfy the needs of the chemists. This accomplishment represents a phase in the study of hallucinogenic plants that must be imitated in the investigation of the chemistry of other narcotics. The laboratory, in this case, became an efficient substitute for nature. By providing suitable conditions, scientists have learned to grow many species in artificial culture.

Cultivation of edible mushrooms is an important commercial enterprise and was practiced in France early in the seventeenth century. Cultivation for laboratory studies is a more recent development.

*Maquira
sclerophylla*

flowering
branch

fruit (1 in.
in diameter)

2-flowered
female

many-flowered
male

RAPÉ DOS INDIOS (*Maquira sclero-phylla;* known also as *Olmedioperebea sclerophylla*) is an enormous tree of the fig family, Moraceae. In the Pariana region of the central Amazon in Brazil, the Indians formerly prepared an hallucinogenic snuff from the dried fruits. The snuff was taken in tribal ceremonials, but encroaching civilization has obliterated its use.

Further studies of this narcotic are needed. The preliminary chemical investigations made so far have not indicated what the active principle may be.

SWEET FLAG (*Acorus calamus*), also called sweet calomel, grows in damp places in the north and south temperate regions. A member of the arum family, Araceae, it is one of two species of *Acorus*. There is some indirect evidence that Indians of northern Canada, who employ the plant as a medicine and a stimulant, may chew the rootstock as an hallucinogen. In excessive doses, it is known to induce strong visual hallucinations. The intoxicating properties may be due to α-asarone and β-asarone, but the chemistry and pharmacology of the plant are still poorly understood.

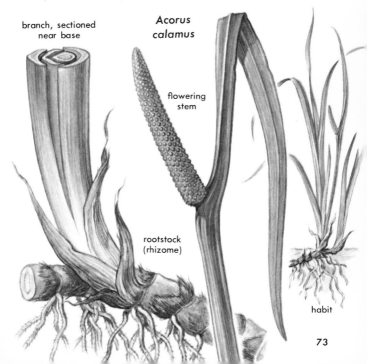

branch, sectioned
near base

*Acorus
calamus*

flowering
stem

rootstock
(rhizome)

habit

Colombian Indians using a snuffing tube fashioned from bird bone.

VIROLAS (*Virola calophylla, V. calophylloidea,* and *V. theiodora*) are among the most recently discovered hallucinogenic plants. These jungle trees of medium size have glossy, dark green leaves with clusters of tiny yellow flowers that emit a pungent aroma. The intoxicating principles are in the blood-red resin yielded by the tree bark, which makes a powerful snuff.

Virola trees are native to the New World tropics. They are members of the nutmeg family, Myristicaceae, which comprises some 300 species of trees in 18 genera. The best known member of the family is *Myristica fragrans,* an Asiatic tree that is the source of nutmeg and mace.

In Colombia, the species most often used for hallucinogenic purposes are *Virola calophylla* and *V. calophylloidea,* whereas in Brazil and Venezuela the Indians prefer *V. theiodora,* which seems to yield a more potent resin.

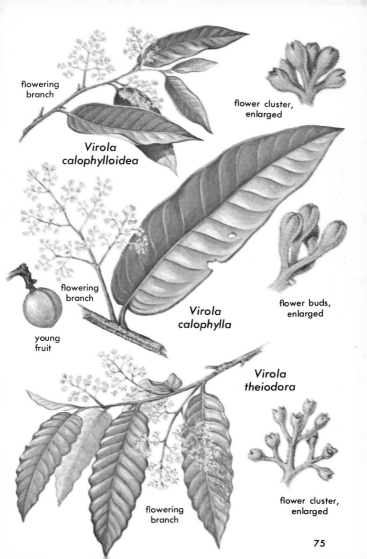

flowering
branch

*Virola
calophylloidea*

flower cluster,
enlarged

flowering
branch

*Virola
calophylla*

flower buds,
enlarged

young
fruit

*Virola
theiodora*

flowering
branch

flower cluster,
enlarged

Strip of bark from *Virola* tree, showing oozing red resin.

AN INTOXICATING SNUFF is prepared from the bark of *Virola* trees by Indians of the northwestern Amazon and the headwaters of the Orinoco. An anthropologist who observed the Yekwana Indians of Venezuela in their preparation and use of the snuff in 1909 commented:

"Of special interest are cures, during which the witch doctor inhales hakudufha. This is a magical snuff used exclusively by witch doctors and prepared from the bark of a certain tree which, pounded up, is boiled in a small earthenware pot, until all the water has evaporated and a sediment remains at the bottom of the pot.

"This sediment is toasted in the pot over a slight fire and is then finely powdered with the blade of a knife. Then the sorcerer blows a little of the powder through a reed . . . into the air. Next, he snuffs, whilst, with the same reed, he absorbs the powder into each nostril successively.

"The hakudufha obviously has a strong stimulating effect, for immediately the witch doctor begins to sing and yell wildly, all the while pitching the upper part of his body backwards and forwards."

Among numerous tribes in eastern Colombia, the use of *Virola* snuff, often called yakee or paricá, is restricted to shamans. Among the Waiká or Yanonamo tribes of the frontier region of Brazil and Venezuela, epena or nyakwana, as the snuff is called, is not restricted to medicine men, but may be snuffed ceremonially by all adult males or even taken occasionally without any ritual basis by men individually. The medicine men of these tribes take the snuff to induce a trance that is believed to aid them in diagnosing and treating illness.

Although the use of the snuff among the Indians of South America had been described earlier, its source was not definitely identified as the *Virola* tree until 1954.

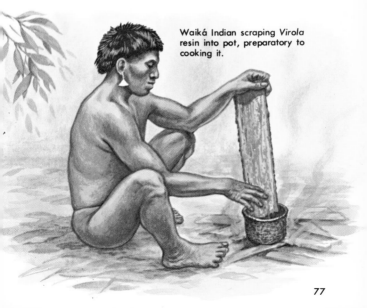

Waiká Indian scraping *Virola* resin into pot, preparatory to cooking it.

PREPARATION OF VIROLA SNUFF varies among different Indians. Some scrape the soft inner layer of the bark and dry the shavings gently over a fire. The shavings are stored for later use. When the snuff is needed, the shavings are pulverized by pounding with a pestle in a mortar made from the fruit case of the Brazil-nut tree. The resulting powder is sifted to a fine, pungent brown dust. To this may be added the powdered leaves of a small, sweet-scented weed, *Justicia,* and the ashes of amasita, the bark of a beautiful tree, *Elizabetha princeps.* The snuff is then ready for use.

Other Indians fell the tree, strip off and gently heat the bark, collect the resin in an earthenware pot, boil

Dried *Justicia* leaves are ground before being added to snuff.

it down to a thick paste, sun-dry the paste, crush it with a stone, and sift it. Ashes of several barks and the leaf powder of *Justicia* may or may not be added.

Still other Indians knead the inner shavings of freshly stripped bark to squeeze out all the resin and then boil down the resin to get a thick paste that is sun-dried and prepared into snuff with ashes added.

The same resin, applied directly to arrowheads and congealed in smoke, is one of the Waiká arrow poisons. When supplies of snuff are used up in ceremonies, the Indians often scrape the hardened resin from arrow tips to use it as a substitute. It seems to be as potent as the snuff itself.

Waiká Indian sifting ground *Justicia* leaves to make fine powder for additive to *Virola* snuff.

A SNUFF-TAKING CEREMONY is conducted annually by many Waiká tribes to memorialize those who have died the previous year. Endocannibalism comprises part of the rite; the ashes of calcined bones of the departed are mixed into a fermented banana drink and are swallowed with the beverage.

The ceremony takes place in a large round house. Following initial chanting by a master of ceremony, the men and older boys form groups and blow huge amounts of snuff through long tubes into each other's nostrils (p. 74). They then begin to dance and to run wildly, shouting, brandishing weapons, and making gestures of bravado. Pairs or groups engage in a strange ritual in which one participant thrusts out his chest and is pounded forcefully with fists, clubs, or rocks by a companion, who then offers his own chest for reciprocation. Although this punishment, in retribution for real or imagined grievances, often draws blood, the effects of the narcotic are so strong that the men do not flinch or show signs of pain. The opponents then squat, throw their arms about each other, and shout into one another's ears. All begin hopping and crawling across the floor in imitation of animals. Eventually all succumb to the drug, losing consciousness for up to half an hour. Hallucinations are said to be experienced during this time.

Waiká round house in clearing in Amazon forest.

EFFECTS OF VIROLA SNUFF are felt within minutes from the time of initial use. First there is a feeling of increasing excitability. This is followed by a numbness of the limbs, a twitching of the face, a lack of muscular coordination, nasal discharges, nausea, and, frequently, vomiting. Macropsia—the sensation of seeing things greatly enlarged—is characteristic and enters into Waiká beliefs about hekulas, the spirit forces dwelling in the *Virola* tree and controlling the affairs of man. During the intoxication, medicine men often wildly gesticulate, fighting these gigantic hekulas.

CAUSE OF THE NARCOTIC EFFECT of *Virola* has been shown by recent studies to be an exceptionally high concentration of tryptamine alkaloids in the resin. Waiká snuff prepared exclusively from the resin of *Virola theiodora* has up to 8 percent of tryptamines, mainly the highly active 5-methoxy-N, N-dimethyltryptamine. Two new alkaloids of a different type—β-carbolines—have also been found in the resin; they act as monoamine oxidase inhibitors and make it possible for the tryptamines to take effect when the resin is taken orally.

OTHER WAYS OF TAKING VIROLA RESIN besides snuffing it are sometimes employed. The primitive nomadic Makú of Colombia often merely scrape resin from the bark of the tree and lick it in crude form. The Witoto, Bora, and Muinane of Colombia prepare little pellets from the resin, and these are eaten when, to practice witchcraft or diagnose disease, the medicine men wish to "talk with the spirit people"; the intoxication begins five minutes after ingestion. There is some vague evidence that certain Venezuelan natives may smoke the bark to get the intoxicating effects.

USE OF VIROLA AS AN ARROW POISON by the Waiká Indians is one of the recent discoveries in the study of curare. The red resin from the bark of *Virola theiodora* is smeared on an arrow or dart, which is then gently heated in the smoke of a fire (shown in the illustration below) to harden the resin. The killing action of the poison is slow. The chemical constituent of the resin responsible for this action is still unknown.

It is interesting that although the arrows are tipped while the hallucinogenic snuff is being prepared from resin from the same tree, the two operations are carried out by different medicine men of the same tribe.

Many other plants are employed in South America in preparing arrow poisons, most of them members of the families Loganiaceae and Menispermaceae.

Waiká Indian holding poison darts in smoky fire to congeal *Virola* resin, applied by dipping or spreading with fingers.

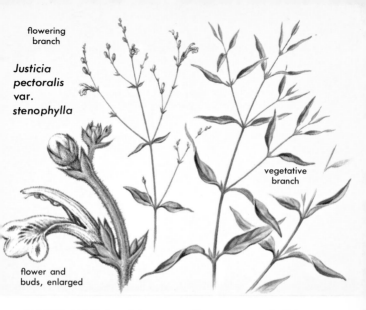

flowering
branch

*Justicia
pectoralis*
var.
stenophylla

vegetative
branch

flower and
buds, enlarged

MASHA-HARI *(Justicia pectoralis* var. *stenophylla)* is a small herb cultivated by the Waiká Indians of the Brazilian-Venezuelan frontier region. The aromatic leaves are occasionally dried, powdered, and mixed with the hallucinogenic snuff made from resin of the *Virola* tree. Other species of *Justicia* have been reported to be employed in that region as the sole source of a narcotic snuff.

Hallucinogenic constituents have not yet been found in *Justicia,* but if any species of the genus is utilized as the only ingredient of an intoxicating snuff, then one or more active constituents must be present. The 300 species of *Justicia,* members of the acanthus family, Acanthaceae, grow in the tropics and subtropics of both hemispheres.

JUREMA (*Mimosa hostilis*) is a poorly understood shrub, the roots of which provide the "miraculous jurema drink," known in eastern Brazil as ajuca or vinho de jurema. Other species of *Mimosa* are also locally called jurema. Several tribes in Pernambuco—the Kariri, Pankarurú, Tusha, and Fulnio—consume the beverage in ceremonies. Usually connected with warfare, the hallucinogen was used by now extinct tribes of the area to "pass the night navigating through the depths of slumber" just prior to sallying forth to war. They would see "glorious visions of the spirit land . . . (or) catch a glimpse of the clashing rocks that destroy souls of the dead journeying to their goal or see the Thunderbird shooting lightning from a huge tuft on his head and producing claps of thunder . . ." It appears, however, that the hallucinogenic use of M. *hostilis* has nearly disappeared in recent times.

Little is known about the hallucinogenic properties of this plant, which was discovered more than 150 years ago. Early chemical studies indicated an active alkaloid given the name nigerine but later shown to be identical with N, N-dimethyltryptamine. Since the tryptamines are not active when taken orally unless in the presence of a monoamine oxidase inhibitor, it is obvious that the jurema drink must contain ingredients other than M. hostilis or that the plant itself must contain an inhibitor in its tissues.

The genus *Mimosa*, closely allied to *Acacia* and *Anadenanthera*, comprises some 500 species of tropical and subtropical herbs and small shrubs. The mimosas belong to the subfamily Mimosoideae of the bean family, Leguminosae. Most of them are American, although some occur in Africa and Asia. Jurema is native only to the dry regions of eastern Brazil.

Mimosa hostilis

flowering branch

single flower, enlarged

85

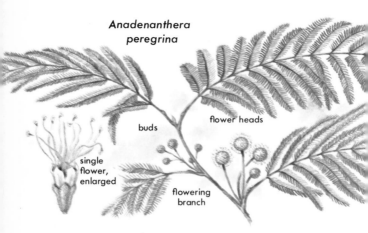

Anadenanthera peregrina

buds

flower heads

single flower, enlarged

flowering branch

YOPO or PARICÁ (*Anadenanthera peregrina* or *Piptadenia peregrina*) is a South American tree of the bean family, Leguminosae. A potent hallucinogenic snuff is prepared from the seeds of this tree. The snuff, now used mainly in the Orinoco basin, was first reported from Hispaniola in 1496, where the Taino Indians called it cohoba. Its use, which has died out in the West Indies, was undoubtedly introduced to the Caribbean area by Indian invaders from South America.

The hallucinogenic principles found in *A. peregrina* seeds include N, N-dimethyltryptamine, N-monomethyltryptamine, 5-methoxydimethyltryptamine, and several related bases. Bufotenine, also present in *A. peregrina* seeds, apparently is not hallucinogenic. Elucidation of the chemical make-up of the seeds of the yopo tree has only recently been accomplished. Future studies may increase our knowledge of the active principle of these seeds.

pods

seeds
("beans")

fruiting branch

THE PREPARATION OF YOPO SNUFF varies somewhat from tribe to tribe. The pods, which are borne profusely on the yopo tree, are flat and deeply constricted between each seed. Gray-black when ripe, the seed pods break open, exposing from three to about ten flat seeds, or beans. These are gathered during January and February, usually in large quantities and often ceremonially. They are first slightly moistened and rolled into a paste, which is then roasted gently over a slow fire until it is dried out and toasted. Sometimes the beans are allowed to ferment before being rolled into a paste. After the toasting, the hardened paste may be stored for later use. Some Indians toast the beans and crush them without molding them into a paste, grinding them usually on an ornate slab of hardwood made especially for the purpose.

Several early explorers described the process. In 1801 Alexander von Humboldt, the German naturalist and explorer, detailed the preparation of yopo by the Maipures of the Orinoco. In 1851, Richard Spruce, an English explorer, visited the Guahibos, another tribe of the Orinoco, and wrote: "In preparing the snuff, the roasted seeds of niopo are placed in a shallow wooden platter that is held on the knee by means of a broad handle grasped firmly with the left hand; then crushed by a small pestle of the hard wood of pao d'arco . . . which is held between the fingers and thumb of the right hand."

The resulting grayish-green powder is almost always mixed with about equal amounts of some alkaline substance, which may be lime from snail shells or the ashes of plant material. Apparently, the ashes are made from a great variety of plant materials: the burned fruit of the monkey pot, the bark of many different vines and trees, and even the roots of sedges. The addition of the ashes probably serves a merely mechanical purpose: to keep the snuff from caking in the humid climate.

The addition of lime or ashes to narcotic or stimulant preparations is a very widespread custom in both hemispheres. They are often added to betel chew, pituri, tobacco, epena snuff, coca, etc. In the case of yopo snuff, the alkaline admixture seems not to be essential. Some Indians, such as the Guahibos, may occasionally take the powder alone. The explorer Alexander von Humboldt, who encountered the use of yopo in the Orinoco 175 years ago, mistakenly stated that ". . . it is not to be believed that the niopo acacia pods are the chief cause of the stimulating effects of the snuff . . . The effects are due to freshly calcined lime." In his time, of course, the presence of active tryptamines in the beans was unknown.

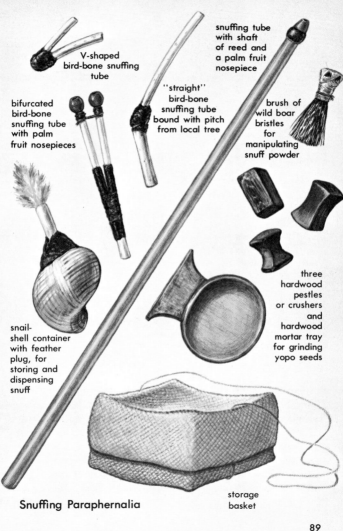

V-shaped bird-bone snuffing tube

snuffing tube with shaft of reed and a palm fruit nosepiece

bifurcated bird-bone snuffing tube with palm fruit nosepieces

"straight" bird-bone snuffing tube bound with pitch from local tree

brush of wild boar bristles for manipulating snuff powder

three hardwood pestles or crushers and hardwood mortar tray for grinding yopo seeds

snail-shell container with feather plug, for storing and dispensing snuff

storage basket

Snuffing Paraphernalia

A yopo tree (*Anadenanthera peregrina*) in Amazonian Brazil. The seeds of this tree are the source of a potent hallucinogenic snuff.

Yopo snuff is inhaled through hollow bird-bone or bamboo tubes. The effects begin almost immediately: a twitching of the muscles, slight convulsions, and lack of muscular coordination, followed by nausea, visual hallucinations, and disturbed sleep. An abnormal exaggeration of the size of objects (macropsia) is common. In an early description, the Indians say that their houses seem to ''. . . be turned upside down and that men are walking on their feet in the air.''

South American Indians of the upper Orinoco´region in characteristic gesticulating postures while under the influence of yopo snuff.

VILCA and SEBIL are snuffs believed to have been prepared in the past from the beans of *Anadenanthera colubrina* and its variety *cébil* in central and southern South America, where *A. peregrina* does not occur. *A. colubrina* seeds are known to possess the same hallucinogenic principles as *A. peregrina* (see p. 86).

An early Peruvian report, dated about 1571, states that Inca medicine men foretold the future by communicating with the devil through the use of vilca, or huilca. In Argentina, the early Spaniards found the Comechin Indians taking sébil "through the nose" to become intoxicated, and in another tribe the same plant was chewed for endurance. Since these Indian cultures have disappeared, our knowledge of vilca snuffs and their use is limited.

Ancient Snuffing Instruments

bird-shaped pottery snuffers; Costa Rica

bone tube; Peruvian coast

reed tube; Bolivia

bamboo tube; Bolivia

snuff tray of carved wood; Bolivian highlands

wooden spatula with handle carved as a fish; Bolivia

wooden mortar and pestle with incised abstract designs; Bolivia

snuff tray with bird-head designs; Bolivia

Cytisus canariensis

branch with young fruits

flowering branches

GENISTA (*Cytisus canariensis*) is employed as an hallucinogen in the magic practices of Yaqui medicine men in northern Mexico. Native to the Canary Islands, the plant was introduced into Mexico. Rarely does any nonindigenous plant find its way into the religious and magic customs of a people. Known also by the scientific name *Genista canariensis*, this species is the "genista" of florists.

Plants of the genus *Cytisus* are rich in cytisine, an alkaloid of the lupine group. The alkaloid has never been pharmacologically demonstrated to have hallucinogenic activity, but it is known to be toxic and to cause nausea, convulsions, and death through failure of respiration.

About 80 species of *Cytisus*, belonging to the bean family, Leguminosae, are known in the Atlantic islands, Europe, and the Mediterranean area. Some species are highly ornamental; some are poisonous.

MESCAL BEAN (*Sophora secundiflora*), also called red bean or coralillo, is a shrub or small tree with silvery pods containing up to six or seven red beans or seeds. Before the peyote religion spread north of the Rio Grande, at least 12 tribes of Indians in northern Mexico, New Mexico, and Texas practiced the vision-seeking Red Bean Dance centered around the ingestion of a drink prepared from these seeds. Known also as the Wichita, Deer, or Whistle Dance, the ceremony utilized the beans as an oracular, divinatory, and hallucinogenic medium.

Because the red bean drink was highly toxic, often resulting in death from overdoses, the arrival of a more spectacular and safer hallucinogen in the form of the peyote cactus (see p. 114) led the natives to abandon the Red Bean Dance. Sacred elements do not often disappear completely from a culture; today the seeds are used as an adornment on the uniform of the leader of the peyote ceremony.

An early Spanish explorer mentioned mescal beans as an article of trade in Texas in 1539. Mescal beans have been found at sites dating before A.D. 1000, with one site dating back to 1500 B.C. Archaeological evidence thus points to the existence of a prehistoric cult or ceremony that used the red beans.

The alkaloid cytisine is present in the beans. It causes nausea, convulsions, and death from asphyxiation through its depressive action on the diaphragm.

The mescal bean is a member of the bean family, Leguminosae. *Sophora* comprises about 50 species that are native to tropical and warm parts of both hemispheres. One species, *S. japonica,* is medicinally important as a good source of rutin, used in modern medicine for treating capillary fragility.

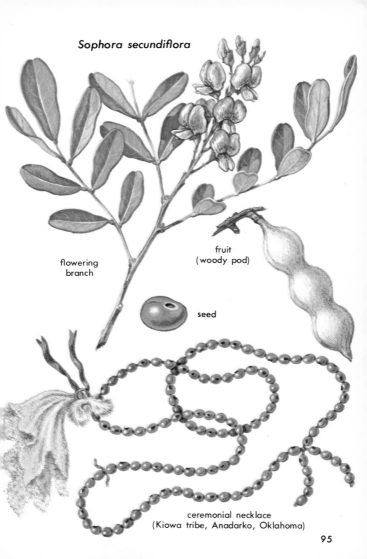

Sophora secundiflora

flowering
branch

fruit
(woody pod)

seed

ceremonial necklace
(Kiowa tribe, Anadarko, Oklahoma)

95

COLORINES (several species of *Erythrina*) may be used as hallucinogens in some parts of Mexico. The bright red beans of these plants resemble mescal beans (see p. 94), long used as a narcotic in northern Mexico and in the American Southwest. Both beans are sometimes sold mixed together in herb markets, and the mescal bean plant is sometimes called by the same common name, colorin.

Some species of *Erythrina* contain alkaloids of the isoquinoline type, which elicit activity resembling that of curare or arrow poisons, but no alkaloids known to possess hallucinogenic properties have yet been found in these seeds.

Some 50 species of *Erythrina*, members of the bean family, Leguminosae, grow in the tropics and subtropics of both hemispheres.

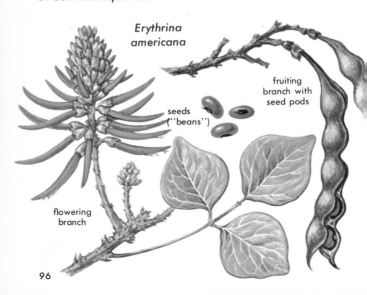

*Erythrina
americana*

fruiting
branch with
seed pods

seeds
("beans")

flowering
branch

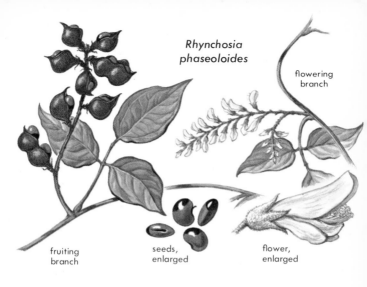

Rhynchosia phaseoloides

flowering branch

fruiting branch

seeds, enlarged

flower, enlarged

PIULE (several species of *Rhynchosia*) have beautiful red and black seeds that may have been valued as a narcotic by ancient Mexicans. What appear to be these seeds have been pictured, together with mushrooms, falling from the hand of the Aztec rain god in the Tepantitla fresco of A.D. 300–400 (see p. 59), suggesting hallucinogenic use. Modern Indians in southern Mexico refer to them as piule, one of the names also applied to the hallucinogenic morning-glory seeds.

Seeds of some species of *Rhynchosia* have given positive alkaloid tests, but the toxic principles have still not been characterized.

Some 300 species of *Rhynchosia*, belonging to the bean family, Leguminosae, are known from the tropics and subtropics. The seeds of some species are important in folk medicine in several countries.

AYAHUASCA and CAAPI are two of many local names for either of two species of a South American vine: *Banisteriopsis caapi* or *B. inebrians*. Both are gigantic jungle lianas with tiny pink flowers. Like the approximately 100 other species in the genus, their botany is poorly understood. They belong to the family Malpighiaceae.

An hallucinogenic drink made from the bark of these vines is widely used by Indians in the western Amazon—Brazil, Colombia, Peru, Ecuador, and Bolivia. Other local names for the vines or the drink made from them are dapa, natema, pinde, and yajé. The drink is intensely bitter and nauseating.

In Peru and Ecuador, the drink is made by rasping the bark and boiling it. In Colombia and Brazil, the scraped bark is squeezed in cold water to make the drink. Some tribes add other plants to alter or to increase the potency of the drink. In some parts of the Orinoco, the bark is simply chewed. Recent evidence suggests that in the northwestern Amazon the plants may be used in the form of snuff. Ayahuasca is popular for its "telepathic properties," for which, of course, there is no scientific basis.

Banisteriopsis caapi

flowering branch

three-winged fruit (triple samara)

single flower, greatly enlarged

99

EARLIEST PUBLISHED REPORTS of ayahuasca date from 1858 but in 1851 Richard Spruce, an English explorer, had discovered the plant from which the intoxicating drink was made and described it as a new species. Spruce also reported that the Guahibos along the Orinoco River in Venezuela chewed the dried stem for its effects instead of preparing a drink from the bark. Spruce collected flowering material and also stems for chemical study. Interestingly, these stems were not analyzed until 1969, but even after more than a century, they gave results (p. 103) indicating the presence of alkaloids.

In the years since Spruce's discovery, many explorers and travelers who passed through the western Amazon region wrote about the drug. It is widely known in the Amazon but the whole story of this plant is yet to be unraveled. Some writers have even confused ayahuasca with completely different narcotic plants.

Colorado Indian from Ecuador rasping the bark of *Banisteriopsis*—a step in preparation of the narcotic ayahuasca drink.

two examples of
pottery vessels
used in
ayahuasca
ceremony

The ceremonial vessel used in the ayahuasca ritual is always hung by the Indians under the eaves at the right side of a house. Although occasionally redecorated, it is never washed.

EFFECTS of drinking ayahuasca range from a pleasant intoxication with no hangover to violent reactions with sickening after-effects. Usually there are visual hallucinations in color. In excessive doses, the drug brings on nightmarish visions and a feeling of reckless abandon. Consciousness is usually not lost, nor is there impairment of the use of the limbs. In fact, dancing is a major part of the ayahuasca ceremony in some tribes. The intoxication ends with a deep sleep and dreams.

An ayahuasca intoxication is difficult to describe. The effect of the active principles varies from person to person. In addition, preparation of the drink varies from one region to another, and various plant additives may also alter the effects.

101

The Yuruparí ceremony in the Colombian Amazon involves ritual ayahuasca intoxication. The Indians are blowing sacred bark flutes.

CEREMONIAL USES of ayahuasca are of major importance in the lives of South American Indians. In eastern Peru, medicine men take the drug to diagnose and treat diseases. In Colombia and Brazil, the drug is employed in deeply religious ceremonies that are rooted in tribal mythology. In the famous Yuruparí ceremony of the Tukanoan Indians of Amazonian Colombia—a ceremony that initiates adolescent boys into manhood—the drug is given to fortify those who must undergo the severely painful ordeal that forms a part of the rite.

The intoxication of ayahuasca or caapi among these Indians is thought to represent a return to the origin of all things: the user "sees" tribal gods and the creation of the universe and of man and the animals. This experience convinces the Indians of the reality of their religious beliefs, because they have "seen" everything that underlies them. To them, everyday life is unreal, and what caapi brings them is the true reality.

CHEMICAL STUDIES of the two ayahuasca vines have suffered from the botanical confusion surrounding them. However, it appears that both species owe their hallucinogenic activity primarily to harmine, the major β-carboline alkaloid in the plants. Harmaline and tetrahydroharmine, alkaloids present in minor amounts, may also contribute to the intoxication. Early chemical studies isolated these several alkaloids but did not recognize their identity. They were given names as "new" alkaloids. One of these names—telepathine—is an indication of the widespread belief that the drink prepared from these vines gave the Indian medicine men telepathic powers.

Harmine   Harmaline

Tetrahydroharmine

Chemical formulas of *Banisteriopsis caapi* and *B. inebrians* alkaloids. Indole nucleus is shown in red.

PLANTS ADDED TO AYAHUASCA by some Indians in the preparation of the hallucinogenic drink are amazingly diverse and include even ferns. Several are now known to be active themselves and to alter effectively the properties of the basic drink. Among these are *Datura suaveolens* (p. 145) and a species of *Brunfelsia* (p. 140)—both members of the nightshade family, Solanaceae, and both containing active principles.

Two additives, employed over a wide area by many tribes, are especially significant. The leaves (but not the bark) of a third species of *Banisteriopsis—B. rusbyana*—are often added to the preparation "to lengthen and brighten the visions." Called oco-yajé in the westernmost Amazon region of Colombia and Ecuador, the liana is cultivated for this purpose, along with *B. caapi* and *B. inebrians*.

Over a much wider area, including Amazonian Brazil, Colombia, Ecuador, and Peru, the leaves of several species of *Psychotria*—especially *P. viridis*—are added. This 20-foot forest treelet belongs to the coffee family, Rubiaceae. Like *B. rusbyana,* it has been found recently to contain the strongly hallucinogenic N, N-dimethyltryptamine.

N, N-Dimethyltryptamine (DMT)

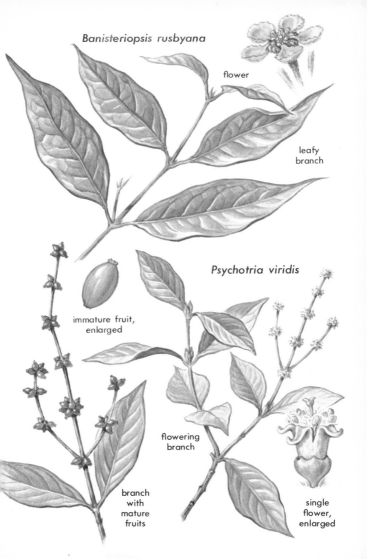

Banisteriopsis rusbyana

flower

leafy branch

Psychotria viridis

immature fruit, enlarged

flowering branch

branch with mature fruits

single flower, enlarged

ANOTHER KIND OF CAAPI is prepared from *Tetrapteris methystica*, a forest vine also belonging to the family Malpighiaceae. One group of Makú Indians of the northwesternmost part of the Brazilian Amazon prepares a cold-water drink from the bark. There is no other plant ingredient. The drink is very bitter and has an unusual yellow hue. This may be the "second kind" of caapi mentioned by several explorers as caapi-pinima, meaning "painted caapi."

Although *T. methystica* produces effects identical with those of *Banisteriopsis caapi*, we still know nothing of its chemistry. However, it is closely related to *Banisteriopsis* and there is every probability that similar or identical alkaloids are present.

There are 90 species of *Tetrapteris*—vines and small trees found throughout the humid American tropics.

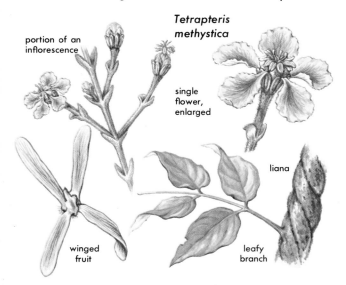

Tetrapteris methystica

portion of an inflorescence

single flower, enlarged

liana

winged fruit

leafy branch

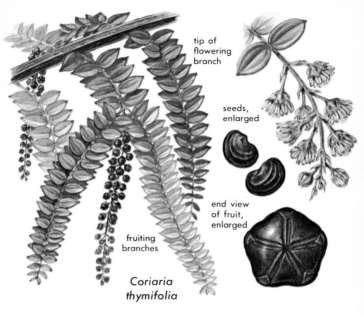

tip of
flowering
branch

seeds,
enlarged

end view
of fruit,
enlarged

fruiting
branches

*Coriaria
thymifolia*

SHANSHI (*Coriaria thymifolia*) is a widespread Andean shrub long recognized as very poisonous to cattle. It has recently been reported as one of the plants used as an hallucinogen by peasants in Ecuador. Shanshi is their name for the plant. The fruits are eaten for their intoxicating effects, which include the sensation of flight. The weird effects are due possibly to an unidentified glycoside, but the chemistry of this species is still poorly understood. Shanshi is one of 15 species of *Coriaria*, most of which are shrubs. They are found in the mountains from Mexico to Chile, from the Mediterranean area eastward to Japan, and also in New Zealand. *Coriaria* is the only known genus in the family, Coriariaceae.

SINICUICHI (*Heimia salicifolia*) is a poorly understood but fascinating auditory hallucinogen of central Mexico. Its leaves, slightly wilted, are crushed and soaked in water. The resulting juice is put in the sun to ferment into a slightly intoxicating drink that causes giddiness, darkening of the surroundings, shrinkage of the world, and drowsiness or euphoria. Either deafness or auditory hallucinations may result, with voices or sounds distorted and seeming to come from a distance. Partakers claim that unpleasant after-effects are rare, but excessive drinking of the intoxicant can be quite harmful.

Sinicuichi is a name given also to other plants that are important both medically and as intoxicants in various parts of Mexico. Other intoxicating sinicuichis are *Erythrina*, *Rhynchosia*, and *Piscidia*, but *Heimia salicifolia* commands the greatest respect. With the closely related *H. myrtifolia*, it has interesting uses in folk medicine. Only in Mexico, however, is the hallucinogenic use important.

Heimia belongs to the loosestrife family, Lythraceae, and represents an American genus of three hardly distinguishable species that range in the highlands from southern United States to Argentina. Presence of hallucinogenic principles was unknown in this family, but chemists have recently found six alkaloids in *Heimia salicifolia*. They belong to the quinolizidine group. One, cryogenine or vertine, appears to be the most active, although the hallucinogenic effects following ingestion of the total plant have not yet been duplicated by any of the alkaloids isolated thus far. This provides us with another example of the often appreciable difference between the effects of drugs taken as natural products and the effects of their purified chemical constituents.

Heimia salicifolia

young fruit

flowering branch

flower bud

variant leaf form

flower, slightly enlarged

seeds, enlarged

109

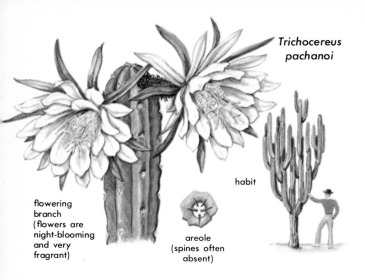

Trichocereus pachanoi

flowering branch (flowers are night-blooming and very fragrant)

areole (spines often absent)

habit

SAN PEDRO (*Trichocereus pachanoi*) is a large colum-nar cactus widely cultivated as an hallucinogen in the Andes of Peru, Ecuador, and Bolivia. The natives, who also call it aguacolla or gigantón, recognize several "kinds," which differ mainly in the number of ribs, the most common type having seven. This cactus is sometimes planted along fields as a fence row to keep sheep and cattle from roaming.

An intoxicating drink called cimora is made from the San Pedro cactus. Short lengths of the stem, often sold in native markets, are sliced like loaves of bread and then boiled in water for several hours, sometimes with superstitious objects such as cemetery dust and powdered bones.

Although cimora is often made from San Pedro alone, several field researchers indicate that a variety of

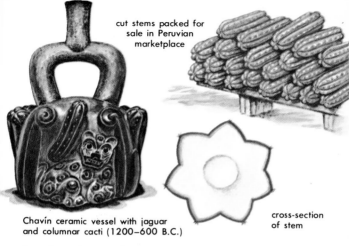

cut stems packed for
sale in Peruvian
marketplace

Chavín ceramic vessel with jaguar
and columnar cacti (1200–600 B.C.)

cross-section
of stem

From collection of Munson-Williams-Proctor Institute—Utica, N.Y.

other plants may sometimes be added to the brew. These
include the cactus *Neoraimondia macrostibas,* an Andean
species the chemistry of which has not yet been determined; the shrub *Pedilanthus tithymaloides* of the cas-
tor oil family; and the campanulaceous *Isotoma longi-
flora.* All these plants may have biodynamic constituents.
On occasion, other more obviously potent plants are
added—*Datura,* for example.

Only recently have researchers become aware
of the importance of the "secondary" plant ingredients often employed by primitive societies. The fact
that mescaline occurs in the San Pedro cactus does not
mean that the drink prepared from it may not be altered
by the addition of other plants, although the significance of the additives in changing the hallucinogenic
effects of the brew is still not fully understood.

Cimora is the basis of a folk healing ceremony that combines ancient indigenous ritual with imported Christian elements. An observer has described the plant as "the catalyst that activates all the complex forces at work in a folk healing session, especially the visionary and divinatory powers" of the native medicine man. But the powers of San Pedro are supposed to extend beyond medicine; it is said to guard houses like a dog, having the ability to whistle in such unearthly fashion that intruders flee in terror.

Although San Pedro is not closely related botanically to peyote, the same alkaloid, mescaline, is responsible for the visual hallucinations caused by both. Mescaline has been isolated not only from San Pedro but from another species of *Trichocereus*. Chemical studies of *Trichocereus* are very recent, and therefore it is possible that additional alkaloids may yet be found in *T. pachanoi*.

Trichocereus comprises about 40 species of columnar cacti that grow in subtropical and temperate parts of the Andes.

There is no reason to suppose that the use of the San Pedro cactus in hallucinogenic and divinatory rituals does not have a long history. We must recognize, certainly, that the modern use has been affected greatly by Christian influences. These influences are evident even in the naming of the cactus after Saint Peter, possibly stemming from the Christian belief that Saint Peter holds the keys to heaven. But the overall context of the ritual and our modern understanding of the San Pedro cult, which is connected intimately with moon mythology, leads us to believe that it represents an authentic amalgam of pagan and Christian elements. Its use seems to be spreading in Peru.

Pachycereus pecten-aboriginum

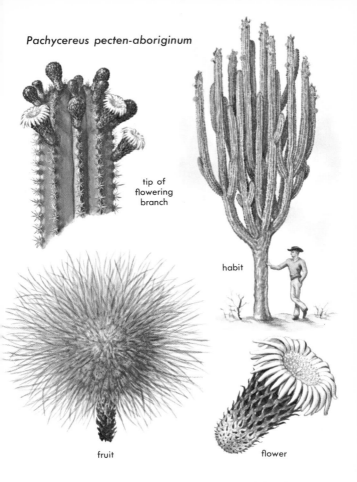

tip of
flowering
branch

habit

fruit

flower

Cawe, or *Pachycereus pecten-aboriginum,* is one of the plants com-
bined with the San Pedro cactus by the Tarahumare of Mexico. It is
not definitely known whether this tall organ cactus is hallucinogenic.

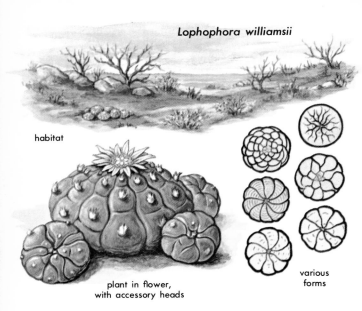

Lophophora williamsii

habitat

plant in flower,
with accessory heads

various
forms

PEYOTE *(Lophophora williamsii),* an unobtrusive cactus that grows in rocky deserts, is the most spectacular hallucinogenic plant of the New World. It is also one of the earliest known. The Aztecs used it, calling it peyotl.

Peyote is a small, fleshy, spineless cactus with a rounded gray-green top, tufts of white hair, and a long carrotlike root. It rarely exceeds 7½ inches in length or 3 inches across. The Indians cut off the crowns to sun-dry into brown, discoidal "mescal buttons" that last long periods and can be shipped to distant points for use. When the top is severed, the plant often sprouts new crowns so that many-headed peyotes are common.

Peyote was first described botanically in 1845 and

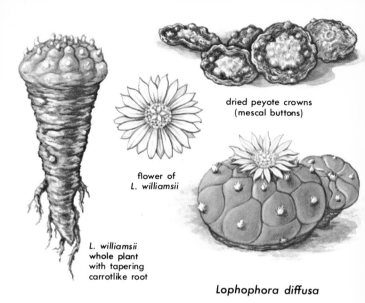

dried peyote crowns
(mescal buttons)

flower of
L. williamsii

L. williamsii
whole plant
with tapering
carrotlike root

Lophophora diffusa

called *Echinocactus williamsii*. It has been given many other technical names. The one used most commonly by chemists has been *Anhalonium lewinii*. Most botanists now agree peyote belongs in a distinct genus, *Lophophora*. There are two species: the widespread *L. williamsii* and the local *L. diffusa* in Querétaro.

Peyote is native to the Rio Grande valley of Texas and northern and central parts of the Mexican plateau. It belongs to the cactus family, Cactaceae, comprising some 2,000 species in 50 to 150 genera, native primarily to the drier parts of tropical America. Many species are valued as horticultural curiosities, and some have interesting folk uses among the Indians.

USE OF PEYOTE BY THE AZTECS was described by Spanish chroniclers. One reported that those who ate it saw frightful visions and remained drunk for two or three days; that it was a common food of the Chichimeca Indians, "sustaining them and giving them courage to fight and not feel fear nor hunger nor thirst; and they say that it protects them from all danger." In 1591, another chronicler wrote that the natives who eat it "lose their senses, see visions of terrifying sights like the devil, and are able to prophesy their future with 'satanic trickery.' "

Dr. Hernández, the physician to the King of Spain, described the cactus as *Peyotl zacatecensis* and wrote of its "wonderful properties." He took note of its small size and described it by saying that "it scarcely issues from the earth, as if it did not wish to harm those who find and eat it." Recent archaeological finds of peyote buttons in the state of Texas are approximately 1,000 years old.

OPPOSITION TO THE USE OF PEYOTE by the Aztecs was strong among the Spanish conquerors. One early Spanish church document likened the eating of peyote to cannibalism. Upset by the religious hold that peyote had on the Indians, the Spanish tried, with great vigor but little success, to stamp out its use.

By 1720, the eating of peyote was prohibited throughout Mexico. But despite four centuries of civil and ecclesiastical persecution, the use and importance of peyote have spread beyond its early limited confines. Today it is so strongly anchored in native lore that even Christianized Indians believe that a patron saint—El Santo Niño de Peyotl—walks on the hills where peyote grows.

There is continuing opposition in certain religious

organizations in the United States to the Indians' use of peyote as a ceremonial sacrament. Nevertheless, the federal government has never seriously questioned or interfered with the practice since it is essentially a religious one. Those tribes living far from sources of peyote—some as far north as Canada—can legally import mescal buttons by mail. Despite constitutional guarantees separating church and state, however, a few states have enforced repressive laws against even the religious use of peyote.

Huichol Indian art indicating the importance of peyote in a trinity involving man and the maize plant.

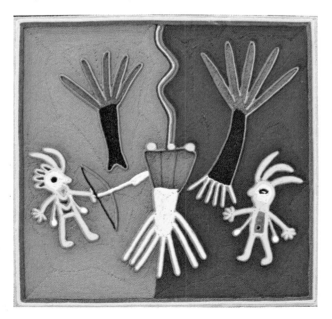

RELIGIOUS IMPORTANCE OF PEYOTE persists among the Tarahumare, Huichol, and other Mexican Indians. The Tarahumare believe that when Father Sun left earth to dwell above, he left peyote, or hikuli, to cure man's ills and woes; that peyote sings and talks as it grows; that when gathered it sings happily in its bags all the way home; and that God speaks through the plant in this way.

Many legends about the supernatural powers of peyote underlie its religious importance. It might be esteemed merely as an everyday medicine, but it has been exalted to a position of near-divinity. The peyote-collecting trip of the Huichols, for example, is highly religious, requiring pilgrims to forego adult experiences, especially sexual, for it reenacts the first peyote quest of the divine ancestors. The pilgrims must confess in order to become spirit and enter into the sacred country through the gateway of clashing clouds, a journey which, according to their tradition, repeats the "journey of the soul of the dead to the underworld."

EFFECTS OF PEYOTE on the mind and body are so utterly unworldly and fantastic that it is easy to understand the native belief that the cactus must be the residence of spirit forces or a divinity. The most spectacular of the many effects is the kaleidoscopic play of indescribably rich, colored visions. Hallucinations of hearing, feeling, and taste often occur as well.

The intoxication may be divided into two periods: one of contentment and extrasensitivity, followed by artificial calm and muscular sluggishness at which time the subject begins to pay less attention to his surroundings and increase his introspective "meditation." Before visions appear, some three hours after eating

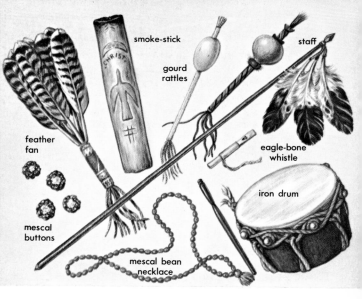

smoke-stick

gourd
rattles

staff

feather
fan

eagle-bone
whistle

iron drum

mescal
buttons

mescal bean
necklace

Paraphernalia used in a typical Plains Indian peyote ceremony. Note the blend of Christian and pagan symbols on the smoke-stick.

peyote, there are flashes and scintillations in colors, their depth and saturation defying description. The visions often follow a sequence from geometric figures to unfamiliar and grotesque objects that vary with the individual.

Though the colored visual hallucinations undoubtedly underlie the rapid spread of the use of peyote, especially in those Indian cultures where the quest for visions has always been important, many natives assert that visions are "not good" and lack religious significance. Peyote's reputation as a panacea and all-powerful "medicine"—both in physical and psychic senses— may be equally responsible for its spread.

USE OF PEYOTE IN THE UNITED STATES first came to public attention about 1880 when the Kiowa and the Comanche Indians established a peyote ceremony derived from the Mexican but remodeled into a vision-quest ritual typical of the Plains Indians. Use of peyote had been recorded earlier, in 1720, in Texas. How the use of peyote diffused from Mexico north, far beyond the natural range of the cactus, is not fully known.

During the 1880's, many Indian missionaries were active in spreading the peyote ceremony from tribe to tribe. By 1920, the peyote cult numbered over 13,000 faithful in more than 30 tribes in North America. It was legally organized, partly for protection against fierce Christian-missionary persecution, into the Native American Church, which now claims 250,000 members. This cult, a combination of Christian and native elements, teaches brotherly love, high moral principles, and abstention from alcohol. It considers peyote a sacrament through which God manifests Himself to man.

THE PEYOTE RITUAL as practiced by Indians in the United States varies somewhat from tribe to tribe. A typical Plains Indian ceremony takes place weekly in an all-night meeting in a teepee. Worshipers sit in a circle around a half-moon altar of sand (see p. 6) on which a large specimen called a "Father Peyote" is set and at which a sacred fire burns. The ashes are shaped into the form of a thunderbird. The ceremony, led by a "roadman," consists of chanting accompanied by rattle and drum, alternating with prayers, lessons, testimonies, and occasionally a curing ritual. At night dried peyote tops (mescal buttons) are moistened and swallowed—from 4 to 30 or more. The ritual ends with breakfast at dawn when the teepee is hauled down.

Indian painting of Peyote "roadman"—leader of the Peyote ceremony. (Original painting is by Stephen Mopope, Kickapoo Indian artist; in collection of Harvard Botanical Museum.)

A PEYOTE VISION was described by a scientist who experienced it as follows: " . . . clouds . . . tail of pheasant turns into bright yellow star; star into sparks. Moving, scintillating screw; hundreds of screws. A sequence of rapidly changing objects in agreeable colors. A rotating wheel in the center of a silvery ground . . . The upper part of a man with a pale face and red cheeks, rising slowly from below. While I am thinking of a friend, the head of an Indian appears. Beads in different colors . . . so bright that I doubt my eyes are closed. . . . Yellow mass like saltwater taffy pierced by two teeth. Silvery water pouring downward, suddenly flowing upward . . . exploding shells turn into strange flowers . . . A drawing of a head turns into a mushroom, then a skeleton in lateral view . . . Head and legs are lacking . . . Soft, deep darkness with moving wheels and stars in . . . pleasant colors. Nuns in silver dress . . . quickly disappearing. Collection of bluish ink bottles with labels. Red, brownish, and violet threads running together in the center. Autumn leaves turning into mescal buttons . . . Man in greenish velvet jumping into a deep chasm. Strange animal turns into a piece of wood in horizontal position."

THE CHEMISTRY OF PEYOTE is extremely interesting and is still subject to intense study by chemists and pharmacologists. More than 30 active constituents have been found in the peyote tissues. They are mainly alkaloids of two types: phenylethylamines and isoquinolines. Much pharmacological and psychological research has been done on mescaline, the alkaloid responsible for the colored visions, but the effects of most of the other constituents, alone or in combination, are not well understood.

CHEMICAL STRUCTURES OF SEVERAL PEYOTE ALKALOIDS

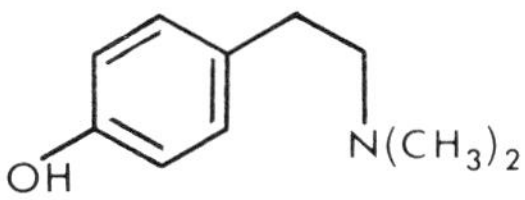

Anhaline

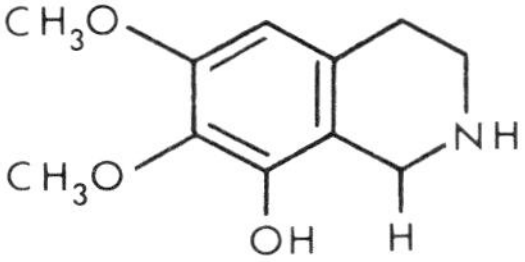

Anhalamine

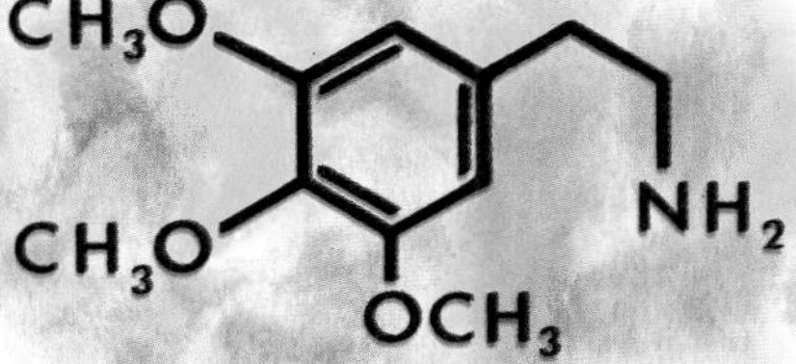

Mescaline

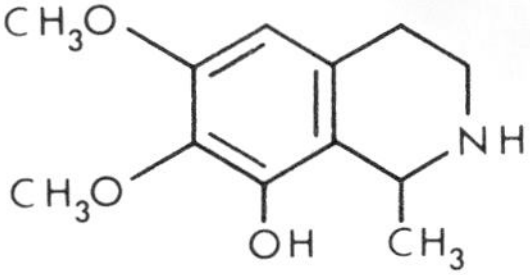

Anhalonidine

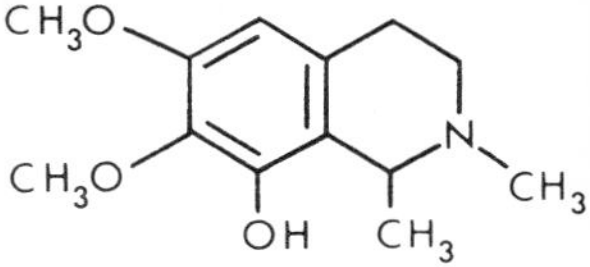

Pellotine

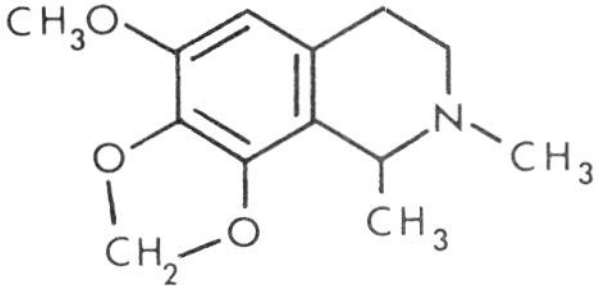

Lophophorine

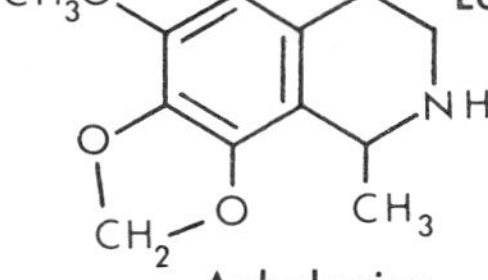

Anhalonine

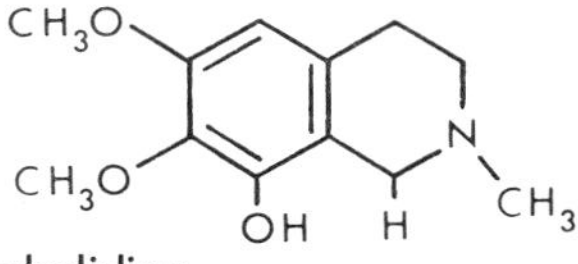

Anhalidine

"FALSE PEYOTES" are other species of cactus used by the Tarahumare and Huichol Indians of northern Mexico. One, called hikuli mulato, is believed to make the eyes so large and clear that the user can see sorcerers. This small cactus has been identified as *Epithelantha micromeris*. A species known as hikuli sunami *(Ariocarpus fissuratus)* is said to be more powerful than peyote (hikuli), and the Tarahumare believe that robbers are powerless to steal when this cactus calls soldiers to its aid.

Hikuli walula saeliami, meaning "hikuli of greatest authority," is so rare that it has not yet been identified,

Epithelantha micromeris

plant in flower,
with
accessory
head

fruits, enlarged

Ariocarpus fissuratus

areoles,
enlarged

but it is reputedly the most powerful of all hallucinogenic cacti. Among the Huichol, tsuwiri (*Ariocarpus retusus*) is considered dangerous to eat; it is believed capable of sorcery and deception, driving a man mad in the desert if he has not been properly instructed by the shaman or is not in a state of ritual purity that allows him to find the true peyote plant.

Nothing is known of the chemistry of *Epithelantha*. Several toxic alkaloids, especially anhalonine, have been found in *Ariocarpus*, but mescaline is apparently absent. *Pelecyphora aselliformis*, another "false peyote," has recently been found to contain alkaloids.

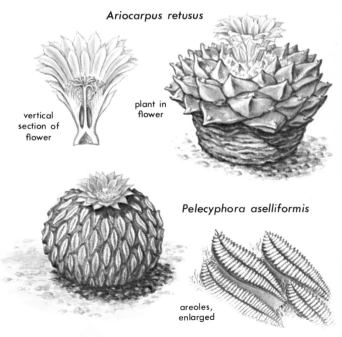

Ariocarpus retusus

vertical section of flower

plant in flower

Pelecyphora aselliformis

areoles, enlarged

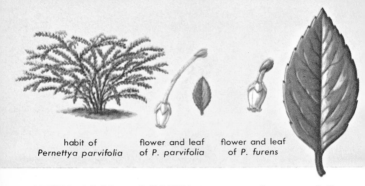

habit of
Pernettya parvifolia

flower and leaf
of P. parvifolia

flower and leaf
of P. furens

HIERBA LOCA and TAGLLI *(Pernettya furens* and *P. parvifolia)* are two of about 25 species of *Pernettya,* mostly very small subshrubs that grow in the highlands from Mexico to Chile, the Galápagos and Falkland islands, Tasmania, and New Zealand. These plants belong to the heath family, Ericaceae, along with the cranberry, blueberry, Scotch heather, rhododendron, and trailing arbutus. Several species are known to be toxic to cattle and man, but only these two are known definitely to be employed as hallucinogens.

Pernettya furens, which in Chile is called hierba loca ("maddening plant") or huedhued, has fruits that, when eaten, can cause mental confusion, madness, and permanent insanity. The intoxication resembles that following the ingestion of *Datura.*

The fruit of taglli, of Ecuador, is well recognized as poisonous, capable of inducing hallucinations and other psychic alterations as well as affecting the motor nerves. Though the chemistry of these and other species of *Pernettya* needs further study, it seems that the toxicity may be due to andromedotoxin, a resinoid, or to arbutin, a glycoside. Both compounds are rather common in this plant family.

Pernettya furens

flowering
branch

fruit,
enlarged

flower,
enlarged

127

SACRED MEXICAN MORNING GLORIES of two species (*Rivea corymbosa* and *Ipomoea violacea*) provide Mexican Indians with hallucinogenic seeds. Although the morning glory family, Convolvulaceae, has been important as the source of several medicines and many ornamentals, only in recent years has it been discovered that some of the 1,700 temperate and tropical species contain highly intoxicating principles. In other parts of the world the concentration of these principles may be higher than in the Mexican morning glories, yet they seem never to have been used as hallucinogens.

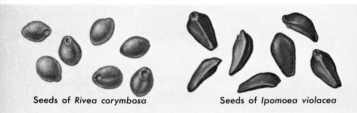

Seeds of *Rivea corymbosa*   Seeds of *Ipomoea violacea*

Shortly after the conquest of Mexico, Spanish chroniclers reported that ololiuqui and tlitliltzin were important divinatory hallucinogens of Aztec religion, magic, and medicine. Ololiuqui is a small, round, brownish seed from a vine, coatl-xoxouhqui ("snake plant"), with heart-shaped leaves and white flowers; tlitliltzin is a black, angular seed. These were recently identified respectively as the seeds of *Rivea corymbosa* and *Ipomoea violacea*. Since botanical nomenclature in this family is not always clear, these two species are sometimes called *Turbina corymbosa* and *Ipomoea tricolor*, respectively. Whereas much was written about ololiuqui, tlitliltzin was merely mentioned in the ancient writings.

MEDICAL AND RELIGIOUS USES of the morning glory called ololiuqui were of major importance to the Aztecs. Ololiuqui is presumed to have pain-killing properties. Before making sacrifices, Aztec priests rubbed themselves with an ointment of the ashes of insects, tobacco, and ololiuqui to benumb the flesh and lose all fear. Hernández, physician to the King of Spain, wrote that "when the priests wanted to commune with their gods and receive messages from them, they ate this plant to induce a delirium, and a thousand visions . . . appeared to them."

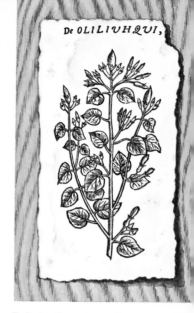

Earliest illustration of *Rivea corymbosa*, also known as ololiuqui (Hernández; Rome, 1651).

One early chronicler wrote that ololiuqui "deprives of his senses him who has taken it, for it is very powerful." Another contended that "the natives communicate in this way with the devil, for they usually talk when drunk with ololiuqui and are deceived by the hallucinations which they attribute to the deity residing in the seeds."

The seeds were venerated and placed in the idols of Indian ancestors. Offerings were made to them under the strictest secrecy in places unknown to persons not involved in the worship.

129

IDENTIFICATION of ololiuqui and tlitliltzin as morning glories had to wait for four centuries, because efforts of the Spanish to eradicate the use of these sacred hallucinogens drove them into the hills. Several crude drawings in the chronicles indicated that ololiuqui was a morning glory. Mexican botanists identified it as such as early as 1854. But doubts persisted because the morning glory family was thought to be devoid of intoxicating principles, and no member of the family had ever been seen employed as an hallucinogen. Mainly on the basis of similarity of the flowers, it was suggested early in the 1900's that ololiuqui was not a morning glory but a *Datura* (p. 142), a known hallucinogen still used in Mexico. Not until 1939 were actual specimens of *Rivea corymbosa* used in Mazatec Indian divinatory rituals collected in Oaxaca and identified as the ololiuqui of the ancient Aztecs. *Ipomoea violacea* was found 20 years later in ceremonial use among the Zapotecs of the same region and identified as tlitliltzin.

An illustration of ololiuqui in fruit, from Sahagún's *Historia de las Cosas de Nueva España*, vol. IV, book XI. Sahagún, a Spanish friar, wrote about the marvels of the New World in the years 1529–1590.

PRESENT USE of the sacred Mexican morning glory seeds differs little from ancient practices. The seeds are used for divination, prophecy, and diagnosis and treatment of illness by many tribes, especially the Chatinos, Chinantecs, Mazatecs, and Zapotecs. In almost all Oaxacan villages, the seeds serve the Indians "as an ever present help in time of trouble."

Indian girl from Oaxaca grinding *Ipomoea* seeds on a metate.

The modern ceremony, featuring the use of morning glory seeds to treat an illness, is a curious blending of old Indian beliefs and Christianity. The native who is to be treated collects the seeds himself. About a thimbleful of the seeds—often the magic number is 13—is measured out. The seeds are ground by a virgin, usually a child, in a special ritual accompanied by complex prayer. Water is added, the resulting beverage is strained, and the patient drinks it at night in silence. After more prayers, he lies down with someone by his side who listens to what he says while intoxicated. This determines the cause of his troubles.

Indian patient drinking potion prepared from *Ipomoea* seeds.

MORNING GLORIES

*Ipomoea
violacea*

var.
Heavenly Blue

var.
Pearly Gates

var.
W

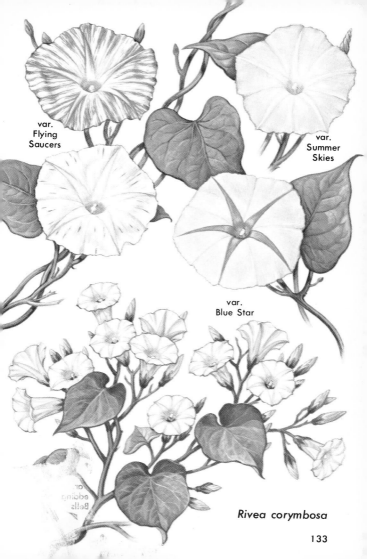

var.
Flying
Saucers

var.
Summer
Skies

var.
Blue Star

Rivea corymbosa

133

EXPERIMENTAL STUDIES of the narcotic morning glories began in 1955 when a psychiatrist published notes on self-experimentation with *Rivea* seeds, showing that they brought on an intoxication accompanied by hallucinations. This announcement prompted chemists to examine the plant, but no active principle could be found until the 1960's. At that time the chemist who discovered LSD analyzed the plant and found several alkaloids closely related to that potently hallucinogenic synthetic compound.

His astonishing discovery met with widespread disbelief, partly because these lysergic-acid derivatives had hitherto been known in nature only in the primitive fungus ergot *(Claviceps purpurea)*, a parasite on the grains of rye. In Europe, when ergot was accidentally ground up in a mill with rye flour and eaten in bread made from the flour, it poisoned whole towns, causing a terrible intoxication and leading frequently to widespread insanity and death. In the Middle Ages, before causes were understood and preventative measures taken, these mysterious mass attacks were called St. Anthony's Fire and were attributed to God's wrath.

Half a dozen of these ergoline alkaloids have been found in seeds of *Rivea corymbosa* and *Ipomoea violacea*. The main hallucinogenic constituents of both seeds are ergine (d-lysergic acid diethylamide) and isoergine, but other related bases occur in minor amounts—chiefly chanoclavine, elymoclavine, and lysergol. The total alkaloid content of *Ipomoea violacea* is five tim s that of *Rivea corymbosa*, which explains why the   s use fewer of the *Ipomoea* seeds in preparin   eir rituals. While these alkaloids are not un   no. numerous morning glories around the world,   only in Mexico have the plants been utilized a

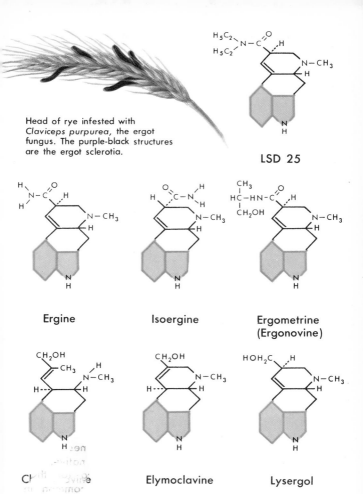

Head of rye infested with
Claviceps purpurea, the ergot
fungus. The purple-black structures
are the ergot sclerotia.

LSD 25

Ergine

Isoergine

Ergometrine
(Ergonovine)

Chanoclavine

Elymoclavine

Lysergol

e sacred Mexican morning glories, showing their chemical
LSD.

MANY HORTICULTURAL VARIETIES of *Ipomoea viola-cea*, including the popular ornamentals Heavenly Blue, Pearly Gates, Flying Saucers, Blue Stars, and Wedding Bells, as well as other varieties of *Ipomoea*, contain hallucinogenic constituents. Other genera, notably *Argyreia* and *Stictocardia*, also contain these substances. The Hawaiian wood rose (*A. nervosa*), for example, has been found to be highly intoxicating. Seeds of *I. carnea*, which are known to possess biodynamic constituents, are said to be used as hallucinogens in Ecuadorian folk medicine. In fact, hallucinogenic compounds are so prevalent in this family, both geographically and botanically, that it is difficult to explain why the morning glories have not been more widely employed as narcotics by primitive societies. Or have they?

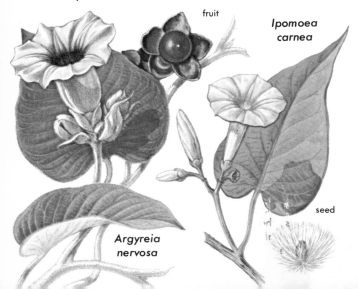

fruit

Ipomoea carnea

seed

Argyreia nervosa

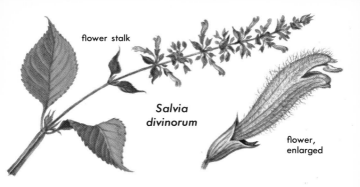

flower stalk

Salvia divinorum

flower, enlarged

HOJAS DE LA PASTORA *(Salvia divinorum)*, of Mexico, is the only one of 700 species of *Salvia* known to be used as an hallucinogen. Mazatec Indians of Oaxaca employ the leaves as a divinatory narcotic, hence divinorum ("of the diviners"). The Mazatecs call the plant hojas de la Pastora in Spanish and shka-Pastora in their native tongue, both names meaning "leaves of the Shepherdess." The leaves are chewed fresh, or the plants are ground on a metate, then diluted with water and filtered for drinking.

The plant is not known in the wild and rarely, if ever, develops from seed. The Mazatecs plant this mint vegetatively in remote mountain ravines, and most families use it as a drug when the sacred mushrooms (p. 58) or morning glory seeds (p. 128) are scarce. It is commonly believed to be the hallucinogenic pipilzintzintli of the ancient Aztecs.

Ingesting leaves of the plant has been found experimentally to induce an intoxication similar to that of the sacred mushrooms but less striking and of shorter duration. It is characterized by three-dimensional colored designs in kaleidoscopic motion. Chemical studies have as yet failed to isolate any psychoactive component.

COLEUS (*Coleus pumilus* and *C. blumei*) is cultivated by the Mazatecs of Oaxaca, Mexico, who reputedly employ the leaves in the same way as they use the leaves of *Salvia divinorum* (see p. 137). Indeed, the Indians recognize the family relationship between these two genera of mints, both of the family Labiatae. They refer to *S. divinorum* as la hembra ("the female") and to *C. pumilus* as el macho ("the male"). There are two forms of *C. blumei,* which they call el niño ("the child") and el ahijado ("the godson").

These two species are native to Asia, where they are valued in folk medicine but apparently have not been used as hallucinogens. No hallucinogenic principle has yet been discovered in the 150 known *Coleus* species.

BORRACHERA (*Iochroma fuchsioides*) is one of about two dozen species of *Iochroma,* all native to the highlands of South America. There are suspicions and unconfirmed reports that several species of *Iochroma* are locally taken in hallucinatory drinks, either alone or mixed with other narcotic plants, by Indians in the Sibundoy Valley of southern Colombia. Although no chemical studies have been made of *Iochroma,* it belongs to the nightshade family, Solanaceae, well recognized for its toxic and hallucinogenic principles.

ARBOL DE LOS BRUJOS ("sorcerers' tree") or latué (*Latua pubiflora*) is used by the Mapuche Indian medicine men of Valdivia, Chile, to cause delirium, hallucinations, and occasionally permanent insanity. There is no cult or ritual surrounding its use, but the tree is ⸱ ly feared and respected. Dosages are a closely guar⸱ ⸱ret, and it is widely believed that a madness of a⸱ ⸱ed duration may be induced by a medicine m⸱ knows

138

Coleus
pumilus

Coleus blumei

Latua
pubiflora

fruit

Iochroma fuchsioides

how to measure the doses properly. The natives employ the fresh fruits.

The alkaloids hyoscyamine and scopolamine have been isolated from the fruit and are responsible for its potent effects. The only species of *Latua* known, the tree is confined to the coastal mountains of central Chile. It belongs to the nightshade family, Solanaceae.

CHIRIC-CASPI and CHIRIC SANANGO *(Brunfelsia)* are the most common of the native names for several species of shrubs that appear to have been important hallucinogens among some South American Indian tribes. The use of the name borrachero, which means "intoxicator," indicates that the natives of Colombia, Ecuador, and Peru recognize the shrub's narcotic properties, and the special care taken in its cultivation seems to suggest a former religious or magic place in tribal life. Recently, real evidence has pointed to the use of several species of *Brunfelsia* either as the source of an hallucinogenic drink, as among the Kachinaua of Brazil, or as an additive to other hallucinogenic

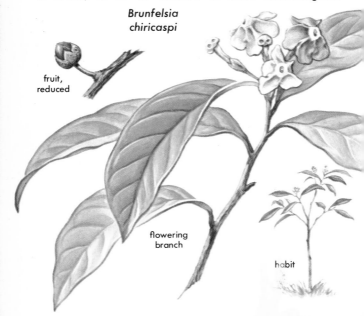

Brunfelsia chiricaspi

fruit, reduced

flowering branch

habit

drinks, as among the Jívaro and Kofán Indians of Ecuador.

The species hallucinogenically employed are *B. grandiflora* and *B. chiricaspi*. All species, however, enter into folk medicine, being used especially to reduce fevers and as antirheumatic agents. *B. uniflora* (as *B. hopeana*) has been included in the Brazilian pharmacopoeia.

Chemical investigation of the active compounds in the various species of *Brunfelsia* is still in the initial stage, and what the active principles may be has not yet been determined. The genus comprises 40 species of shrubs native to tropical South America and the West Indies. It belongs to the nightshade family, Solanaceae.

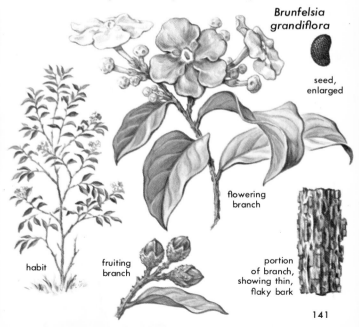

Brunfelsia grandiflora

seed, enlarged

flowering branch

habit

fruiting branch

portion of branch, showing thin, flaky bark

DATURAS *(Datura)* form a genus of some 20 species of the nightshade family, Solanaceae. They occur and are used as hallucinogens in both hemispheres. The drug is usually prepared by dropping pulverized seeds into fermented drinks or by steeping leaves and twigs in water. Use differs widely from tribe to tribe.

Intoxication caused by the drug is characterized initially by effects so violent that physical restraint must be imposed until the partaker passes into a stage of sleep and hallucinations. The medicine man interprets the visions as visitations of the spirits and is supposedly thus able to diagnose disease, apprehend thieves, and prophesy the future.

Some of the Indians in the Andes of southern Colombia cultivate a number of clones of highly atrophied "varieties," perhaps incipient species. They may be the result of mutations induced by viruses. Biological monstrosities, their identification to species is often difficult. Medicine men maintain that they differ in potency from the usual *Daturas*, an indication that perhaps their chemical constitution as well as their morphology has been changed. They seem to be confined to Sibundoy, a mountain-girt valley in the high Andes of Colombia.

Basically, all species of *Datura* have a similar chemical composition. Their active principles are mainly hyoscyamine and scopolamine, which are tropane alkaloids. Scopolamine is often the major constituent. A number of minor, chemically related alkaloids may be present: atropine, norscopolamine, meteloidine. The differences among species are chiefly in the relative concentrations of these various alkaloids. Though highly toxic, most species have been used extensively in medicine from early times to the present. Their use in folk medicine derives from their high concentration of alkaloids.

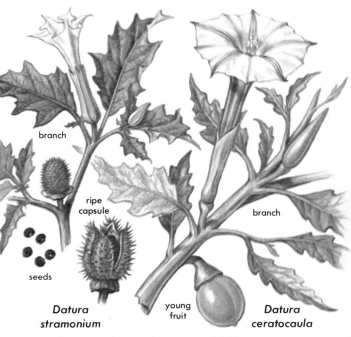

branch

ripe
capsule

seeds

*Datura
stramonium*

young
fruit

branch

*Datura
ceratocaula*

JIMSON WEED or thorn apple (*Datura stramonium*) is an ill-scented weedy annual with white to purplish flowers. Probably native to North America, it now grows in temperate and sub-tropical regions around the world. All parts of the plant, especially the brownish-black seeds, are toxic. This species is believed to have been the chief ingredient of wysoccan, used by the Algonquin Indians of eastern North America before the ritual of initiation into manhood (see p. 9).

TORNA-LOCO (*Datura cerato-caula*) is a fleshy plant with thick, forking stems that grows in marshes and shallow waters. Its unusual habitat and its strong narcotic properties earned it a special place among the ancient Mexican hallucinogens. The Aztecs, who invoked its spirit in treating certain diseases, referred to it as "sister of ololiuqui," one of the morning glories (see p. 128). Its modern Mexican name, torna-loco ("maddening plant"), indicates its potency as a narcotic.

TOLOACHE (*Datura inoxia;* known also as *D. meteloides*), a coarse, climbing annual native to Mexico and southwestern United States, has a long history of use as an hallucinogen. It was extremely important to the Aztecs, who called it toloatzin. Hernández recorded many medical uses but warned that taken in excess it would drive a patient to madness.

The modern Tarahumares still add the roots, seeds, and leaves to their maize beer. Zunis value the plant as a narcotic, an anesthetic, and a poultice for treating wounds. Only the rain priests are permitted to gather it. The priests put the powdered root in their eyes; also they chew the root to commune with spirits of the dead, asking intercession for rain.

The Luiseños use an infusion of toloache in an initiation ceremony. The young participants who drink it dance, screaming like animals, until they drop and succumb to the drug's effects. Yumans take it to induce dreams, gain occult powers, and predict the future. Yokuts use the drug in a spring ceremony to assure good health and long life to the young. The related *D. discolor* and *D. wrightii* of the same region are similarly used.

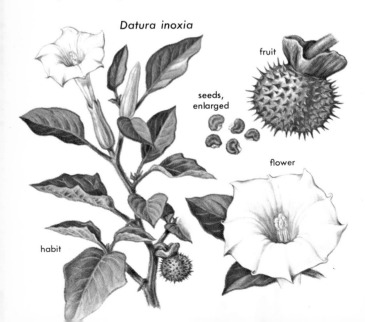

Datura inoxia

fruit

seeds, enlarged

flower

habit

TREE DATURAS of several species are native to South America where they go by such native names as borrachero, campanilla, maicoa, floripondia, huanto, toé, and tanga. All are cultivated plants, unknown in the truly wild state and associated with man since earliest times.

Datura suaveolens is indigenous to the warmer lowlands. Recognized as toxic and narcotic, it is used as an hallucinogen, alone or as an admixture. The northern Andes, from Colombia to Peru, appears to be the center of the group's origin. Species from this region are *D. arborea, D. aurea, D. candida, D. dolichocarpa, D. sanguinea,* and the newly discovered *D. vulcanicola* (see pp. 146–147 for examples).

Aboriginal peoples from Colombia to Chile value these trees as sources of ritualistic hallucinogens and medicines. In Chile, the Mapuche Indians use *D. candida* and *D. sanguinea* to correct unruly children. The Jívaros say that the spirits of their ancestors admonish recalcitrant children during the hallucinations. The ancient Chibchas of Bogotá used *D. aurea* seeds to induce stupor in the wives and slaves of dead warriors and chieftains before they were buried alive to accompany husbands and masters on the last trip.

At Sogamoza, Colombia, Indians took *D. sanguinea* ceremonially in the Temple of the Sun. The narcotic prepared from this red-flowered species is known locally as tonga. Many Peruvian natives still believe that tonga permits them to communicate with ancestors or other departed souls. In Matucanas, Peru, Indians say it will reveal to them treasures preserved in ancient graves, or huacas, hence the local name for the plant—huacacachu ("grave plant"). The tree daturas are sometimes considered a distinct genus: *Brugmansia.*

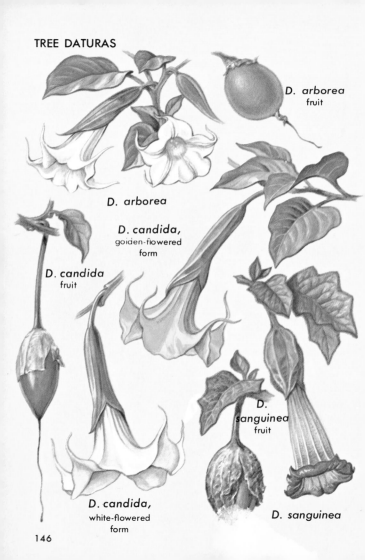

TREE DATURAS

D. arborea
fruit

D. arborea

D. candida,
golden-flowered
form

D. candida
fruit

*D.
sanguinea*
fruit

D. candida,
white-flowered
form

D. sanguinea

146

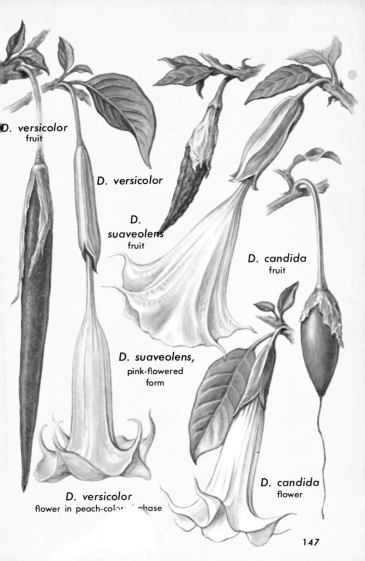

D. versicolor
fruit

D. versicolor

D. suaveolens
fruit

D. candida
fruit

D. suaveolens,
pink-flowered
form

D. versicolor
flower in peach-colored phase

D. candida
flower

147

Sibundoy Indian witch doctor collecting leaves and flowers of *Methysticodendron amesianum*. Perhaps nowhere in the New World does the importance of hallucinogens in native magic and medicine acquire such significance as in the Valley of Sibundoy, which has been characterized as "the most narcotic-conscious area of the New World."

CULEBRA BORRACHERO *(Methysticodendron amesianum)*, a tree reaching a height of 25 feet, is known only from cultivated trees in the Kamsá Indian town of Sibundoy, Colombia. The Indians also call it mitskway borrachera ("snake intoxicant").

This tree is the only species of its genus and may represent an extremely aberrant form of a tree species of *Datura*. Its 11-inch white flowers differ from those of the tree daturas in having their bell-shaped corolla split nearly to the base.

An infusion of the leaves is said to be more potent and dangerous to use than similar preparations of *Datura*. The chemical composition explains its great potency: 80 percent of the several typical tropane alkaloids present is scopolamine. Even in small doses, this drug may cause excitement, hallucinations, and delirium. The trees are the special property of certain medicine men who employ the drug in difficult cases of disease diagnosis, divination, prophecy, or witchcraft.

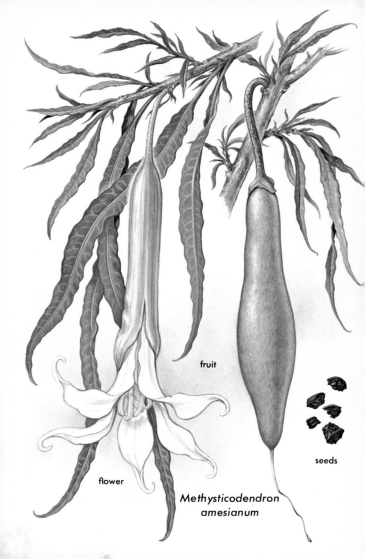

flower

fruit

seeds

Methysticodendron
amesianum

SHANIN (*Petunia violacea*) is one of the most recently reported hallucinogens. It is taken by the Indians in Ecuador to induce the sensation of flight. Although an alkaloid of unknown identity has been reported from this species of petunia, phytochemical investigation of petunias is urgently needed.

Some 40 species of petunias grow in South America and in warmer parts of North America. Members of the nightshade family, Solanaceae, they are closely allied to the genus *Nicotiana* (tobacco). *Petunia violacea* as well as other species are horticulturally important. Cultivated varieties, with their attractive, funnel-shaped blooms, are popular garden flowers that bloom profusely throughout the summer months.

KEULE (*Gomortega keule*) is a small tree restricted to about 100 square miles in central Chile. It is the only species in a rare family, Gomortegaceae, related to the nutmeg family. The Mapuche Indians of Chile are said to eat the fruit of keule, or hualhual, for intoxication, but whether the effects are truly hallucinogenic is not yet known. So far, there have been no chemical studies made of this tree.

TAIQUE (*Desfontainia hookeri*) is a shrub of Andean valleys. Its leaves, made probably into a tea, are employed in southern Chile as a folk medicine and as a narcotic. Whether their effects are truly hallucinogenic is not known, nor has their chemical composition been investigated. The genus *Desfontainia* contains one or two other Andean species and belongs to the family Desfontainiaceae. A related family, Loganiaceae, includes the plants from which certain South American arrow poisons are made.

*Petunia
violacea*

*Gomortega
keule*

budded
branch

fruiting
branch

*Desfontainia
hookeri*

TUPA (*Lobelia tupa*), a tall, variable plant of the high Andes, is also called tabaco del diablo ("devil's tobacco"). In Chile, the Mapuche Indians smoke the dried leaves of this beautiful red-flowered plant for their narcotic effects. Whether they are truly hallucinogenic has not yet been established. They contain the alkaloid lobeline and several derivatives of it. The same alkaloid occurs in some North American species of *Lobelia,* especially *L. inflata,* known locally as Indian tobacco. It has been used medicinally and as a smoking deterrent. There are 300 species of *Lobelia,* mostly tropical and subtropical, and they belong to the bluebell family, Campanulaceae. Some are highly prized as garden ornamentals.

ZACATECHICHI (*Calea zacatechichi*), an inconspicuous shrub ranging from Mexico to Costa Rica, is a recently discovered hallucinogen that seems to be used only by the Chontals of Oaxaca. They take it to "clarify the senses" and to enable them to communicate verbally with the spirit world. From earliest times, the plant's intensely bitter taste (zacatechichi is the Aztec word meaning "bitter grass") has made it a favorite folk medicine for fevers, nausea, and other complaints.

After drinking a tea made from the shrub's crushed dried leaves, an Indian lies down in a quiet place and smokes a cigarette made of the dried leaves. He knows that he has had enough when he feels drowsy and hears his own pulse and heartbeat. Recent studies indicate the presence of an unidentified alkaloid that may be responsible for the auditory hallucinations.

There are a hundred or more species of *Calea.* They belong to the daisy family, Compositae, and grow on open or scrubby hillsides in tropical America. Some species enter into folk medicine.

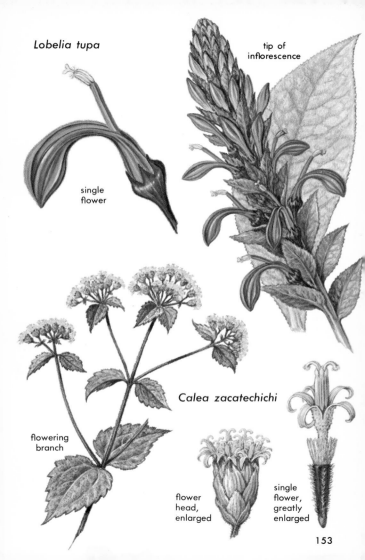

Lobelia tupa

tip of
inflorescence

single
flower

Calea zacatechichi

flowering
branch

flower
head,
enlarged

single
flower,
greatly
enlarged

153

PSYCHOPHARMACOLOGY

Psychopharmacology studies the effects of drugs, especially hallucinogens, on the central nervous system.

The effects of psychoactive agents result from constituents that belong to many classes of chemicals. All have one characteristic in common: they are biodynamic, affecting normal metabolism of the animal body.

Hallucinogens act directly on the central nervous system, but they may also affect other parts of the body. They have both physical and psychic activity. Their effects are usually short-lived, lasting only as long as the chemical remains at the point of action in the body. Pseudohallucinations—often indistinguishable to the layman from true hallucinations—may be caused by many abnormal conditions upsetting body homeostasis, or normal metabolism: fevers, fasting, lack of water for long periods, poisons, etc. Pseudohallucinations may often be of much longer duration than hallucinations.

If a plant contains an active substance, its medical potential is of interest to pharmacologists. Investigation may indicate that true hallucinogenic compounds have value for purposes far removed from their psychoactivity. An example is scopolamine, an alkaloid of the nightshade family. Taken in proper doses, it intoxicates, inducing a state between consciousness and sleep and characterized by hallucinations. Scopolamine, however, has medical uses not associated with the central nervous system: it is antispasmodic and antisecretory, mainly in the alimentary canal and urinary tracts.

Some psychiatrists believe that mental disorders are the result of an imbalance in body chemistry: "For every twisted thought, there is a twisted molecule." Some specialists formerly thought and still maintain that "model

Crayon drawing
by a Tukanoan Indian
of Amazonian Colombia,
depicting one of the
images experienced during
an aboriginal caapi intoxication.
Collected in the field
by the Colombian
anthropologist Dr. Gerardo
Reichel-Dolmatoff, who studied
the mythological significance
of hallucinogens
among the Indians.

psychoses''—artificially induced states similar to some abnormal mental conditions—might be a valuable analytic tool. There are many similarities between psychotic conditions, such as schizophrenia, and the mental state induced by hallucinogens. Whether or not the use of hallucinogens to create such model psychoses will be of therapeutic value is still a question, but there is little doubt that hallucinogens may be of experimental help in understanding the functioning of the central nervous system. One specialist states that studies of ''various aspects of the normal and the abnormal'' may elucidate certain areas of the ''hinterland of character.''

It must be remembered that alteration of the function of the central nervous system by chemicals is not new; it is older than written history. In the past, especially in primitive societies, hallucinogens were employed in magico-religious and curing rituals, rarely for pleasure.

In some cultures, notably those suffering acculturation, hallucinogens are sometimes used to enhance social contacts or even for explaining mental disorders. If we compare uses of hallucinogenic plants in primitive societies with the medical value claimed for them by some psychiatrists, we see that model psychoses are not a new development. Artificially induced psychoses have long been used as healing practices in primitive cultures.

Although many modern psychiatrists are critical of chemical psychoses as tools in treating mental aberrations, it is too early completely to rule out their possible medical value.

OTHER HALLUCINOGENIC PLANTS

In addition to the hallucinogenic plants used by primitive peoples, numerous other species containing biodynamic principles are known to exist. Many are common household varieties like catnip, cinnamon, and ginger. No reliable studies have been made of the hallucinogenic properties of such plants. Some of the effects reported to have been caused by them may be imaginary; other reports may be outright hoaxes. Nevertheless, many of these plants do have a chemistry theoretically capable of producing hallucinations. Experimentation continues with plants—common and uncommon—known or suspected to be hallucinogenic, and new ones are continually being discovered.

MORE INFORMATION

Cooper, John M., "Stimulants and Narcotics," in HANDBOOK OF SOUTH AMERICAN INDIANS, J. H. Seward (Ed.), Bureau of American Ethnology, Bulletin No. 143, U.S. Government Printing Office, Washington, D.C., 1949

Efron, D. H. (Ed.), ETHNOPHARMACOLOGIC SEARCH FOR PSYCHOACTIVE DRUGS, Public Health Service Publ. No. 1645, U.S. Government Printing Office, Washington, D.C., 1967

Emboden, William J., Jr., NARCOTIC PLANTS, Macmillan Co., New York, 1972

Harner, N. J., HALLUCINOGENS AND SHAMANISM, Oxford University Press, New York, 1973

Hartwich, C., DIE MENSCHLICHEN GENUSSMITTEL, Chr. Herm. Tauchnitz, Leipzig, 1911

Heim, R., and R. Gordon Wasson, LES CHAMPIGNONS HALLUCINOGÈNES DU MEXIQUE, Edit. Mus. Hist. Nat., Paris, 1958

Hoffer, A., and H. Osmund, THE HALLUCINOGENS, Academic Press, New York, 1967

Keup, W., DRUG ABUSE—CURRENT CONCEPTS AND RESEARCH, Charles C. Thomas, Publisher, Springfield, Ill., 1972

Lewin, Louis, PHANTASTICA—NARCOTIC AND STIMULATING DRUGS: THEIR USE AND ABUSE, Routledge and Kegan Paul, London, 1964

Pelt, J.-M., DROGUES ET PLANTES MAGIQUES, Horizons de France, Strasbourg, 1971

Safford, William E., "Narcotic Plants and Stimulants of the Ancient Americans," in ANNUAL REPORT OF THE SMITHSONIAN INSTITUTION, 1916, Washington, D.C., 1917

Schleiffer, H., SACRED NARCOTIC PLANTS OF THE NEW WORLD INDIANS, Hafner Press, New York, 1973

Schultes, Richard Evans, "The Botanical and Chemical Distribution of the Hallucinogens," in ANNUAL REVIEW OF PLANT PHYSIOLOGY, 21, 1970.

Schultes, Richard Evans, and Albert Hofmann, THE BOTANY AND CHEMISTRY OF HALLUCINOGENS, Charles C. Thomas Publisher, Springfield, Ill., 1973

Taylor, Norman, FLIGHT FROM REALITY, Duell, Sloan and Pearce, New York, 1949

Wasson, R. Gordon, SOMA, DIVINE MUSHROOM OF IMMORTALITY, Harcourt, New York, 1967

INDEX

Front cover, clockwise from lower left: fly agaric mushroom, sinicuichi, morning glory, tree datura, peyote, cannabis. **Back cover,** see page 62.